Pers[...]

in the

Province of Pennsylvania

1740 — 1773

Excerpted and Reprinted from
Pennsylvania Archives, Series 2. Volume II

Indexed Edition

John B. Linn
and
William H. Egle

08-1941

CLEARFIELD

Excerpted and Reprinted from
Pennsylvania Archives, Series 2. Volume II

Reprinted
Genealogical Publishing Company
Baltimore, 1967

Reprinted for
Clearfield Company by
Genealogical Publishing Co.
Baltimore, Maryland
1991, 1995, 1997, 2005, 2007

Library of Congress Catalogue Card Number 66-28670

ISBN-13: 978-0-8063-0213-3
ISBN-10: 0-8063-0213-5

Made in the United States of America

PERSONS NATURALIZED IN PENNSYLVANIA.

PENSILVANIA, }
SECRETARY'S OFFICE. }

In pursuance of An Act of Parliament made in the thirteenth year of the Reign of his present Majesty King George, the second, Entitled An Act for naturalizing such Foreign Protestants, and others therein mentioned, as are settled or shall settle in any of his majesties Colonies in America.

At a Supreme Court held at Phil'd'a for the Province of Pennsylvania, Before Jeremiah Langhorne, Thomas Græme and Thomas Griffiths, Esqrs., Judges of the said Court, the 25th, 26th & 27th days of September, in the year of our Lord one thousand seven Hundred & Forty, between the Hours of Nine & Twelve of the Clock in the Forenoon of the same Days, the following Persons, being Foreigners and having inhabited and resided the space of seven years and upwards in his Majesty's Colonies in America, and not having been absent out of some of the said Colonies for a longer space than two months, at any one time, during the said seven years, and having produced to the said Court Certificates of their having taken the Sacrament of the Lord's Supper in some Protestant or Reformed Congregation in this Province within three months before the said Court, Took & Subscribed the Oaths, and did make and repeat the Declaration prescribed by the said Act, to entitle them to the Benefit thereof, and thereby became Natural born Subjects of Great Britain, as the same is Certified into this office by the Judges of the said Court, viz:

Persons' names.	Of what place.	Time of taking the Sacrament.
Peter Kock,	Philad'a City,	Aug. 10th, 1740
John Mason,	do.	Sept. 23, 1740
Gustavus Hesselius,	do.	do.
Frederick Smith,	do.	do.
Andrew Reinberg,	Phil'a County,	do.
Jacob Hoffman,	do.	Sept. 22d, 1740
John George Meyer,	do.	do.
Jacob Bryer,	Bucks Co.,	June 29th, 1740
Michael Fersler,	do.	Sept. 21st, 1740
Jacob Server,	do.	Sept. 22d, 1740
Joannes Bartholomew Rieger, Lutheran Minister,	} Lancaster Co.,	Sept. 19th, 1740

Persons' names.	Of what place.	Time of taking the Sacrament.
John William Straube,	Phil'a County,	Sept. 21st, 1740
Jacob Arent,	do.	Sept. 22d, 1740
Andreas Bernhard,	do.	June 29th, 1740
Jacob Arwogaust,	Bucks Co.,	do.
Oswald Walt,	Phil'a County,	do.
Leonard Melihar,	do.	Sept. 22, 1740
Adam Kittler,	do.	Aug. 3, 1740
George Bergstraser,	Bucks Co.,	Sept. 22, 1740
George Henry Hartsle,	do.	do.
John Frey,	do.	do.
George Beck,	Philad'a Co.,	Sept. 25th, 1740
Christopher Aukenbrand,	do.	do.
John Rody,	Bucks,	Sept. 22d, 1740
Blessius Byar,	Phil'a City,	do.
John Wendell Breikbill,	do.	Sept. 7, 1740
Bartholomeus Hornbergher,	Bucks,	Sept. 11th, 1740
Peter Rule,	do.	Sept. 22, 1740
Peter Gruber,	do.	Sept. 11th, 1740
George Hartsell,	do.	Sept. 22, 1740
Dedrick Rudey,	do.	do.
Philip Henrick Seller,	do.	do.
Joseph Penkick,	Philad'a County,	Sept. 25, 1740
George Reiger,	do.	July 15th, 1740
Casper Simon,	do.	July 29th, 1740
Uriah Humble, Jun.,	Bucks,	Sept. 25th, 1740
Andrew Trumbole,	Philad'a County,	June 29th, 1740
John George Kepler,	do.	Sept. 1st, 1740
Hans Bernhard Kepler,	do,	July 29th, 1740
Michael Sebastain,	do.	Sept. 1st, 1740
Hieronimus Hans,	do.	Sept. 25, 1740
Henrick Hans,	do.	Sept. 1st, 1740
George Roup,	Bucks,	July 22, 1740
Mathias Otto,	Phil. County,	Sept. 1, 1740
Valentine Geygar,	do.	Sept. 25th, 1740
Peter Roup,	Bucks,	July 22d, 1740
John Levick,	do.	do.
Elias Hasell,	do.	do.
Jacob Keefer,	do.	do.
Mathias Pender,	Phil. Co.,	Sept. 25th, 1740
John Frederick Richard,	do.	do.
Balthazar Sailor,	do.	Sept. 1st, 1740
Jacob Walter,	do.	Sept. 7th, 1740
Martin Humble,	Bucks,	Sept. 25th, 1740
Peter Ritter,	Phil. Co.,	Sept. 1st, 1740

Persons' names.	Of what place.	Time of taking the Sacrament.
Bartholomew Maul,	Phil. Co.,	Sept. 23, 1740
John Vogler,	do.	do.
Mattheus Nees,	Phil'a County,	Sept. 21, 1740
John Philip Streeter, Lʊth'n Minister,	} Bucks County,	do.
Henrick Ritter,	do.	Sept. 11th, 1740
Henry Schleydorn,	Phil'a City,	Aug. 3rd, 1740
Mathias Shutz,	do.	July 30, 1740
Mathias Schutz, Jun'r,	do.	Aug. 3rd, 1740
John Leonard Stone,	Phil'a County,	July 6th, 1740
Adam Reder,	do.	Sept. 22d, 1740
Valentine Keeler,	do.	do.
Lenard Knopp,	Bucks,	do.
Hendrick Peters,	Phil'a Co.,	do.
Nicholas Coob, jun'r,	do.	Sept. 25th, 1740
Henry Mathison,	Phil'a City,	July 27, 1740
John Michael Dill,	do.	July 26th, 1740
George Albright,	do.	Aug. 3d, 1740
Felix Fesler,	do.	Sept. 23, 1740
Jacob Uttrey,	do.	Sept. 7th, 1740

And at the same Court, the following Persons being Quakers, or such who conscientiously scruple to take an Oath, being also Foreigners, and having complied with the terms required by the afores'd Act of Parliament, Took & Subscribed the Qualifications for them appointed by the same Act of Parliament; viz. :

Persons' names.	Of what place.
John Cressman,	Philad'a County.
Henry Ott,	Bucks Co.
John George Vanlear,	Chester Co.
Benjamin Rosenbergh,	Phil'a Co.
Isaac Miller,	do.
Christian Snider,	do.
Lodowick Harmony,	do.
John Vanfossen,	do.
John Shelliberger,	do.
Christopher Trewbey,	Bucks Co.
Mathias Nice,	Phil'a Co.
Christian Stowfer,	do.
Henry Stettler,	do.
Dewald Nice,	Bucks.
Philip Redwal,	Philad'a Co.
John Hunter,	do.
Michael Ryer,	do.
Gerrart Shrager,	do.

Persons' names.	*Of what place.*
Gossen Shrager, Jun'r,	Philad'a Co.
Andrew Fisher,	do.
Michael Ritter,	do.
Isaac Grall,	Phil'a Co.
George Wood,	do.
Johannes Snider,	do.
Nicholas Walber,	Bucks.
Barthol Writter,	Phil'a Co.
Daniel Warley,	do.
Anthony Hunter,	do.
Jacob Peters,	do.
Peter Peters,	do.
Valentine Keeler,.	do.
Henry Goothouse,	Lancaster Co.
John Philip Shellig,	Phil'a Co.
Jacob Huber,	Lancaster Co.
Henrick Hermell,	Phil'a Co.
Jacob Collman,	do.
Abraham Sailer,	do.
Anthony Gilbert,	do.
Jacob Naglee,	do.
Abraham Kintzing,	Phil'a City.
George Hows,	Phil'a Co.
George Shorn,	do.
Daniel Berndaller,	Phil'a Co.
Herman Gotshall,	do.
Blassius Daniel Mackiñel,	do.
Casper Ott,	Bucks Co.
Alexander Dibbindurfer,	do.
John Groothouse,	Phil'a Co.
Jacob Souter,	do.
Martin Wightman,	Lancaster.
George Bensell,	Phil'a Co.
Charles Bensell,	do.
Nicholas Rabine,	do.
Philip Sharp,	do.
Valentine Shadaire,	do.
Adam Leberger,	do.
John Gull,	do.
Casper Feight,	do.
Paul Wykerline,	do.
John Omstadt,	do.
Peter Snider,	Bucks Co.
Garret Rattenhausen,	Phil'a Co.
John Bartholomew,	do.

Persons' names.	Of what place.
John Wood,	Phil'a Co.
Mark Minser,	do.
John George Hoffman,	do.
Bernard Woolfinger,	do.
Baltes Rezer,	do.
George Crossman,	do.
Jno. George Little John,	Bucks.
Henry Bard,	Phil'a Co.
Casper Wister,	Phil'a City.
Joseph Smith,	Phil'a Co.
John Heiser,	do.
John Rush,	do.
Thomas Myer,	Phil'a City.
John Wistar,	do.
Arent Hassert,	do.
David Deshler,	do.

[At a Supreme Court held at Philadel'a for the Province of Pennsilvania, Before Jermiah Langhorne, Thomas Græme & Thomas Griffitts, Esqu'rs, judges of the said court the tenth & eleventh days of April, in the year of our Lord, one thousand seven hundred and forty-one.]

Persons' names.	Of what place.	Time of taking the Sacrament.
John Philip Behm,	Philad'a Co.,	April 11th, 1741
Henrich Warner,	do.	do.
Sebastian Graaff,	do.	Feb. 10th, 1740
Johan Dedrick Youngman,	do.	April 11th, 1741
George Honig,	Lancaster Co.,	April 10th, 1741
Feight Georger,	Phil'a Co.,	Ap. 6th, 1741
John George Merstaller,	Bucks Co.,	Ap. 2d, 1741
Johan Dedrick Buckert,	Phil. Co.,	Ap. 11th, 1741
George Jacob Spingler,	do.	Feb. 4th, 1740
Paul Linsenbekler,	do.	Ap. 7th, 1741
Andreas Overbeck,	do.	Ap. 5th, 1741
Christopher Smith,	do.	do.
Henry Rumfeldt,	Bucks Co.,	Ap. 2d, 1741
Johannes Shafer,	Philad'a Co.,	Ap. 7th, 1741
Theowald Bawm,	do.	Feb. 4th, 1740
Henrick Dewald,	do.	Ap. 11th, 1741
Conrad Niedermardt,	Chester Co.,	Mar. 29th, 1741
Adam Eichely,	Phil. Co.,	Ap. 11th, 1741
Francis Roos,	do.	Apr. 5th, 1741
Johannes Kastner,	Lancaster Co.,	Ap. 11th, 1741
Christian Leamon,	Phil. Co.,	Ap. 5th, 1741
Johan Adam Schrocker,	do.	Ap. 2d, 1741

Persons' names.	Of what place.	Time of taking the Sacrament.
Charles Hunter,	Phil. Co.	Feb. 5th, 1740
Valentine Berndheisell,	do.	Ap. 11th, 1741
Ulrick, Stephen,	do.	Ap. 5th, 1741
Jacob Frye,	do.	Ap. 7th, 1741
Jacob Miller,	do.	Mar. 31, 1741
Hans Michael Crumryne,	do.	Ap. 9, 1741
Johannes Neihawsen,	do.	Ap. 11th, 1741
Stephen Brecht,	Lancaster Co.,	do.
John Jost Heck.	do.	do.

Certified by

THO. GRÆME,
THOMAS GRIFFITTS.

PHILADELPHIA, *May 7th*, 1741.

The foregoing is a true & perfect list taken from the orginal Certificate, under the Hands of Thomas Græme and Thomas Griffitts, Esqr's, remaining in my office.

PAT. BAIRD, *Secretary*,

[At a Supream Court held at Philadelphia, for the Province of Pensilvania, Before Thomas Græme & Thomas Griffitts, Esq'rs, two of the Judges of the said court, the twenty-fourth day of Sept'r, in the year of our Lord one thousand seven hundred forty-one.]

Persons' names.	Of what place.	Time of taking the Sacrament.
John Casper Stoever,	Lancaster Co.,	Sep. 20th, 1741
Conrad Sharff,	do.	Sep. 13th, 1741
Nathaniel Lytner,	do.	Sep. 20th, 1741
Michael Rhyne,	do.	do.
Elias Long,	Philad'a Co.,	Aug. 30th, 1741
Martin Reyer,	do.	do.
Bartle Cooker,	do.	do.
Peter Balsbach,	Lancaster Co.,	Sep. 22d, 1741
Jöhannes Gorner,	do.	Sep. 13th, 1741
Lawrence Lawfer,	Philad'a Co.,	Aug. 30th, 1741
Philip Reid,	do.	do.
George Wellker,	do.	do.
Hans Adam Mayrer,	do.	Aug. 23d, 1741
Benedict Straum,	do.	Aug. 30th, 1741
Johannes Dunckell,	Phila'a Co.,	Sep. 16th, 1741
Ulrick Sherer,	do.	Sep. 15th, 1741
Hans George Kapple,	do.	Sep. 24th, 1741
Michael Reder,	do.	Aug. 30th, 1741
Henrick Hoover,	do.	Sep. 21st, 1741

Persons' names.	Of what place.	Time of taking the Sacrament.
Henrick Gollman,	Phila'a Co.	Aug. 30th, 1741
Johannes Tricktenhengst,	do.	Sep. 16th, 1741
Peter Beysell,	do.	Aug. 23, 1741
Jacob Frederick Reiger,	Lancaster Co.,	Sep. 13th, 1741
George Zimmerman,	Phil. Co.,	Aug. 30th, 1741
Henrick Klein,	Lancaster,	Aug. 13th, 1741
John Bishop,	do.	Sep. 24th, 1741
Philip Emmert,	Phil. Co.,	Aug. 16th, 1741
George Paltsgraaff,	do.	do.
Jacob Kraus,	do.	Sep. 16th, 1741
Certified by		

THO. GRÆME,
THOMAS GRIFFITTS.

And in like manner, in April Term following, to wit: On the Tenth day of April, 1742, at the said Supream Court, before said Judges, in pursuance of the foresaid Act of Parliament, the following persons being Foreigners & under the same circumstances with those mentioned in the foregoing Certificate, took & subscribed the Oaths and did make & repeat the Declaration aforesaid according to the directions of the Act of Parliament aforesaid; and thereby became natural born subjects of Great Britain, as the same is certified into this office by the Judges of the said Court, viz:

Persons' names.	Of what place.	Time of taking the Sacrament.
Christian Markling,	Philad'a Co.,	Mar. 23d, 1741
Nicholas Kern,	Bucks Co.,	Mar. 9th, 1741
Peter Frachsell,	do.	do.
Peter Frachsell, Jun'r,	do.	do.
Abraham Woolring,	do.	Feb. 20th, 1741
Certified by		

THO. GRÆME,
THOMAS GRIFFITTS.

PHILADELPHIA, *April 24th*, 1742.

The foregoing are true and perfect Lists taken from the original Certificates under the Hands of Tho. Græme and Thomas Griffitts, Esq'rs, remaining my office.

[At a Supream Court held at Philadelphia, for the Province of Pennsylvania, Before Thomas Græme and Thomas Griffitts, Esq'rs, Judges of the said Court, the Twenty-fourth day of September, in the year of our Lord one thousand seven hundred and forty-two.]

Persons' names.	Of what place.	Time of taking the Sacrament.
Peter Ulrich,	Philad'a Co.,	1742, Sep. 19.
Frederick Antes,	do.	" " 12.
Johan Peter Walber,	Bucks Co.,	" " 5.
Certify'd by		

THO. GRÆME.

The foregoing is a true and perfect List taken from the original Certificate, under the Hand of Thomas Græme, Esq'r, remaining in my office.

RICHARD PETERS, *Secr'y.*

(Philad'a, June 21st, 1743, sent to London.)

[At a Supream Court held at Philadelphia, for the Province of Pennsylvania, Before John Kinsey, Thomas Græme and William Till, Esq'rs, Judges of the said Court, the Eleventh, Twelfth and Thirteenth Days of April, in the year of our Lord one thousand seven hundred and forty-three.]

Persons' names.	Of what place.	Time of taking the Sacr ament.
Hans Adam Ox,	Philadelphia Co.,	Jan. 25th, 1742
Leonard Ox,	do.	April 3d, 1743
Johan Michael Weichell,	do.	do.
John Brown,	do.	do.
Michael Knoll,	do.	Apr. 10th, 1743
Michael Kalb	do.	do.
Simon Belzener,	do.	do.
George Hilig,	do.	Feb. 12th, 1742
Johan Martin Derr,	do.	Apr. 3d, 1743
Jacob Keitzmiller,	Lancaster Co.,	do.
Leonard Buck,	Philad'ia Co.,	do.
Wendell Swegger,	Lancaster Co.,	do.
Michael Rauch,	do.	do.
Michael Brubagh,	do.	do.
John Derved Darfer,	do.	do.
John Smose,	Lancaster Co.,	Apr. 3d, 1743
Jacob Keller,	do.	do.
Adam Miller,	do.	do.
George Sailor,	Philad'a Co.,	April 5th. 1743
Nicholas Steyler,	Bucks County,	April 5th, 1743
Peter Walber,	do.	April 4th, 1743
Hans George Overbeck,	Philadelphia Co.,	April 3rd, 1743
Adam Stump,	Lancaster Co.,	do.
Hendrick Moyer,	do.	April 5th, 1743
Leonard Crow,	do.	do.
Jacob Kough,	Philadia. Co.,	Feb. 3d, 1742
John Deany,	do.	April 9th, 1743

Persons' names.	Of what place.	Time of taking the Sacrament.
George Meyer,	Philadia. Co.,	April 4th, 1743
Andreas Mayz,	Bucks Co.,	April 9th, 1743
Philip Stior,	Lancaster Co.,	April 3d, 1743
David Beehler,	do.	do.
Leonard Miller,	do.	do.
Jacob Wise,	do.	do.
Jacob Wise, Jun.,	do.	do.
John Berger,	do.	do.
Sebastian Reyer,	do.	do.
Michael Heintz,	Philad'a Co.,	April 4th, 1743
Michael Heintz, Jun.,	do.	do.
Anthony Heintz,	Bucks Co.,	do.
Peter Conradt,	Philad'a Co.,	Jan. 25th, 1742
Jacob Mawrer,	do.	April 3rd, 1743
Frederick Mawrer,	do.	do.
Conrad Templeman	Lancaster Co.,	April 4th, 1743
Mathias Ringer,	Philad'a Co.,	April 9th, 1743
George Shultz,	do.	April 4th, 1743
Johan Peter Koogher,	Lancaster Co.,	April 3rd, 1743
Bernhard Renn,	Philad'a Co.,	April 10th, 1742
Peter Heybey,	do.	April 3rd, 1743
Henry Chriest,	do.	do.
Lawrence Bast,	do.	do.
Ulrick Burkhalter,	Bucks Co.,	April 4th, 1743
Conradth Border,	Philad'a Co.,	April 5th, 1743
John Nicholas Mertz,	do.	do.
Michael Hooffman,	Bucks Co.,	April 4th, 1743
Henry Circle,	Philad'a Co.,	April 4th, 1743
Michael Kraps,	do.	April 10th, 174
Henry Kraps,	do.	do.
Simon Kraps,	do.	do.
Johannes Mickendurfer,	Bucks Co.,	April 3rd, 1743
Jacob Fellman,	Philad'a Co.,	do.
John George Evensidell,	do.	April 4th, 1743

And at the same Court, the following Persons being Quakers, or such who Conscientiously scruple to take an oath, being also Foreigners, and having complied with the Terms required by the aforesaid Act of Parliament, took and subscribed the Qualifications for them appointed by the same Act of Parliament, &c., viz:

Persons' names.	Of what place.
John Zimmerman, *alias* Carpenter,	Lancaster Co.
John Bucher,	do.
John William Crox	Philad'a Co.

Persons' names.	Of what place.
Henry Ottman,	Philad'a Co.
Henry Whetstone,	do.
Nicholas Harmany,	do.
Conrad Fisher,	do.
Joseph Albright,	Bucks Co.
Abraham Ashman,	Philada. Co.
George Kelkner,	do.
Henrick Reezer,	Lancaster Co.
William Reezer,	do.
Ulrick Reezer,	Bucks Co.
Johannes Kyme,	Philada. Co.
Johan Geo. Stoneman,	do.
John Stineman,	do.
Frederick Fandy,	Germantown.
Valentine Cressmore,	Philad'a Co.
Jacob Shaid,	Bucks Co.
John Lesher,	Philad'a Co.
Mathias Beck,	do.
William Speck,	do.
Michael Kelkner	do.
Ingle Peter,	Philad'a Co.
Abraham Peter,	do.
Gabriel Bowyer,	do.
Peter Rodermell,	do.
Christian Stump,	Lanct'r Co.
Michael Nett,	do.
Michael Nett, Jun'r,	do.
Elias Wagonar,	Philad'a Co.
Gabriel Iseberger,	do.
Florain Boobinger,	do.
Geo. Adam Widenar,	do.
David Wiser,	do.
Sebastian Cimmerman,	do.
Daniel Lewan,	do.
John Perdo,	do.
Philip Faust,	do.
Sebastian Wagoner,	Chester Co.
Dedrick Peydleman,	Philad'a Co.
Jacob Karst,	Philad'a City.
Sebastian Derr,	Bucks Co.
Philip Schmyer,	do.
Philip Beyer,	Philad'a Co.
John Lyne,	Lanc'r Co.
Reinard Vogdes,	Philad'a Co.
Christopher Weifer,	do.

Persons' names.	Of what place.
William Greanmore,	Philad'a Co,
George Casper Shleher.	do.
Abraham Bartolet.	do.
John Bartlet, Jun'r,	do.
Jacob Vetter,	do.
Christian Brower,	Chester Co.
Peter Brecker,	Lanc'r Co.
Adam Widenar,	Philad'a Co,
John Widtner,	do.
John Geo. Widtner,	do.
Michael Spoon,	do.
Martin Kindig,	Lanc'r Co.
John Kindig,	do.
William Pott,	do.
Abraham Shelley.	Bucks Co.
Lawrence Slaymaker,	Lanc'r Co.
Jacob Graff,	do.
Christian Kintrin,	Philad'a Co.
Johannes Baldt,	do.
Jacob Baldt,	do.
Rudolph Marolff,	do.
Charles Kress,	do.
Sebastian Miller,	do.
Christian Tappan,	Lanc'r Co.
Emanuel Sasmanhausen,	Philad'a Co.
Johannes Leddraugh,	do.
George Beighley,	do.
Jacob Tatwiler,	Bucks Co.
Andreas Leddraugh,	Philad'a Co.
Peter Dunkleberry,	do.
John Lingenfelter,	Lancaster Co.
Jacob Wise,	Philad'a Co.
Jacob Kalkgleeser,	Germantown, in Phil'a. Co.
Emanuel Kalkgleeser,	do.
Abraham Bryder,	Bucks Co.
Jacob Wislar,	Philad'a Co.
Jacob Mast,	Lanc'r Co.
John Accree,	Phil'a Co.
John Adams,	do.
Christian Allebach,	do.
Collee Hefflefinger,	do.
Casper Bowman,	do.
Daniel Stouffer,	do.

20—Vol. II.

Persons' names.	Of what place
Valetine Kratz,	Phil'a Co.
Peter Beidler,	do.
Jacob Buckwalter,	do.
Ulrick Beidler,	do.
Isaac Meyer,	do.
Johannes Brewer,	Chester Co.
Ulrick Sherrer,	Phil'a Co.
Jacob Clemens,	do.
Hans Meyer.	Phil'a Co.
Andreas Swartz,	do.
Lawrence Cornelius,	do.
Henry Hefflefinger	do.
Nicholas Uplinger,	do.
Nicho's Haldeman, Jun'r,	do.
Nicho's Haldeman,	Chester Co.
Christian Beidler,	Philad'a Co.
Abraham Fluri,	do.
John Beyle,	do.
Jacob Bussart,	Chester Co.
Peter Ash,	do.
Henry Rudht,	Philad'a Co.
Johannes Brandt,	do.
Jacob Landtes,	do.
Johannes Bekner,	do.
Johannes Swing,	do.
Jacob Krop,	do.
Jacob Graffe,	do.
Hans Wyerman,	do.
Hans Wyerman, Jun'r,	de.
Jacob Wierman.	do.
Jacob Greder,	do.
Christian Halderman,	do.
Henry Rosyberger,	do.
Jacob Overholser,	do.
Jacob Overhalser, Jun'r,	do.
John Winer,	Philad'a Co.
Jacob Engars,	Chester Co.
Johannes Engars,	do.
Jost Engar,	do.
Jacob Landes, Jun'r,	Phi'a Co.
Michael Dirstein,	Bucks Co.
Conrad Stemm,	Philad'a Co.
Abraham Meyer,	do.
Julius Kassle,	do.
Johannes Kassle,	do.

Persons' names.	Of what place.
Hans Ulrick Burgher,	Philad'a Co.
Jacob Shoemaker,	do.
Jacob Hogman,	Philad'a Co.
Samuel Mussleman,	do.
Jacob Hafflefinger,	do.
Philip Hough,	do.
Jacob Bach,	Chester Co.
Jacob Landes,	Philad'a Co.
Jacob Sable Kool,	Bucks Co.
Jacob Overholster,	Philad'a Co.
Henry Overholtzer,	do.
John Bower,	do.
Samuel Bower,	do.
Henry Dentlinger,	do.
Julius Julius,	do.
Christian Meyer,	do.
John Henry Snyder,	do.
Abraham Meyer,	do.
Peter Shelbert,	do.
Johannes Stump,	Lancaster Co'ty.
Christian Myer, Jun'r,	Philad'a Co.
Hans Reiff,	do.
Jacob Sessenning,	Lanc'r Co'ty.
Francis Ladshower,	Philad'a Co.
Peter Mell,	do.
Johannes Steiner,	Chester Co.
John Clemens,	Philad' Co.
Frederick Alderfer,	do.
Hans Ulrick Stober,	do.
Martin Greter,	do.
John Kiem,	do.
Nicholas Englehort,	do.
Henry Wenger,	do.
George Reezer,	Chester Co.
Christian Crall,	Bucks Co.
Jacob Huntsberger,	Philad'a Co.
Frederick Styner,	Philad'a Co.
Andreas Hoffman,	Chester Co.
Anthony Noble,	of the City Philadelphia, Painter.
Peter Swartz,	Philad'a Co.
Johannes Mak,	of Germantown, Phil'a Co.
Andreas Buzzard,	Philad'a Co.
Christian Brandiman,	do.

Persons' names.	*Of what place.*
Johannes Seigler,	Philad'a Co.
Peter Bingamon,	do.
Christopher Reinwald,	do.
Valentine Baker,	Lancaster Co.
Michael Krider,	Philad'a Co.
George Dresher,	do.
Christo'r Dresher,	do.
George Kribell,	do.
George Heidrig,	do.
Abraham Heidrick,	do.
Hans Hubner,	do.
Christopher Moll,	do.
Leonard Hendricks,	do.
Paul Hendricks,	do.
Wendal Wyand,	do.
Casper Kribell,	do.
David Seibt,	do.
Johannes Heanes,	do.
Jost Shingler,	do.
Christopher Weigner,	do.
Christian Lehman,	of Germantown, Phil'a Co.
John Lehman,	do.
Christopher Yeacle,	do.
Abraham Yakell,	do.
Baltazar Hendrick,	do.
John Hubener, Jun'r,	Philad'a Co.
Abraham Yackell,	do.
Christopher Yakell,	do.
John Yakell,	Bucks Co
Balthazar Yakell,	do.
David Meeshter,	Philad'a Co.
George Shultz,	do.
Balthazar Haus,	Bucks Co.
William Smith.	Philad'a Co.
Martin Hildebridle,	do.
John George Wambelt	Bucks Co.
Andrew Hawk,	Philad'a Co.
Jacob Levan,	do.
Conrad Heninger,	do.
George Scholtz. Jun'r,	do.
Melchior Scholtz,	do.
Christopher Scholtz,	do.
John Mock,	do.
Melchior Weigner,	do.

Persons' names.	Of what place.
Abraham Beyer, Jun'r,	Philad'a Co.
Hans Weigner,	do.
Christopher Noyman,	do.
William Caricis,	do.
Nicholas Moritz,	do.
Herman Junghen,	do.
Henry Lukenbeel,	do.
Henry Grubb,	do.
Conrad Grubb,	do.
Michael Kuntz,	do.
John Hallman,	do.
Frederick Baker,	do.
Johannes Shinnholser,	Chester Co.
Jacob Swartz,	Bucks Co.
Christopher Bastian,	Philad'a Co.
Lodowick Englehort,	do.
Dewald Kemp,	do.
Johannes Quartstillwag,	Bucks Co.
Peter Federolfe,	Philad'a Co.
Paul Branner,	do.

Certified by

JOHN KINSEY, *Ch. Just.*

The foregoing is a true and perfect List, taken from the original Certificate, under the Hands of John Kinsey, Esq'r, remaining in my Office.

RICHARD PETERS, *Secr'y.*

PHILADELPHIA, 21st June, 1743.

(Copy sent to the Secretary of the Lords of Trade.)

[At a Supream Court held at Philadelphia for the Province of Pennsylvania, Before John Kinsey, Thomas Græme and William Till, Esq'rs, Judges of the said Court, the twenty-fourth, Twenty-sixth and Twenty-seventh Days of September, in the year of our Lord one thousand seven hundred and forty-three.]

Persons' names.	Of what place.	Time of taking the Sacrament.		
John Cunrad Radd,	Philadelphia Co..	September	11th,	1743
John Jacob Rathe,	do.	do.		
Michael Bettley,	Lancaster Co.,	September	18th.	1743
Mathias Higner,	Philadelphia Co..	do.		
Michael Haninger,	do.	do		
Johannes Schreyck,	Lancaster Co..	July	3rd,	1743
Melcher Ingel,	do.	August	21st,	1743
Jacob Myer,	Bucks Co..	September	18th,	1743
Adam Hill,	Philadelphia Co.,	August	21st,	1743

Persons' names.	Of what place.	Time of taking the Sacrament.
Gotliff Hill,	Lancaster Co.,	September 21st, 1743
Henry Acker,	Bucks Co.,	September 16th, 1743
Michael Moll,	Philad'a Co.,	September 18, 1743
Bernard Hubbley,	Lancaster Co.,	do.
Jacob Smith,	Philadelphia Co.,	do.
Burchard Hofman,	do.	September 11th, 1743
Getty Grimm,	Bucks County,	Septem'r 19th, 1743
Christopher Exline,	Philad'ia Co.,	May 25th, 1743
Melchior Susholt,	do.	September 11th, 1743
Christopher Stadler,	Bucks Co.,	Sept. 16th, 1743
Philip Jacob Ackre,	do.	Sept. 19th, 1743
George Staningar,	do.	do.
Henry Ricke,	do.	do.
John Liechtinwallner,	do.	do.
Jacob Sneffle,	Lancaster Co.,	Sept. 18, 1743
Casper Shaffner.	do.	{ Taken in the presence of John Hanniberger & Jacob Kook, as by their Depositions appear.
Peter Knopple,	do.	{ Taken as by the above, two persons Depositions appear.
Hans Jacob Kunts, John Hanniberger,	do.	{ Taken by them, as by ye Depositions of Peter Knopple & Casper Shaffner appear.

And at the same Court, the following Persons being Quakers, or such who Conscientiously scruple to take an Oath, being also Foreigners, and having comply'd with the Terms required by the aforesaid Act of Parliament, and an Act of General Assembly of the Province of Pennsylvania, made, in the year of our Lord 1742, Took and subscribed the Qualifications for them appointed by the same Act of Parliament, &ca., vizt:

Persons' names.	Of what place.
Henry Kendrick,	Lancaster Co.
Jacob Beyer,	do.
Rudolph Stoner,	do.
Andrew Musseman,	do.
Christian Musseman,	do.
Jacob Harnest,	do.
John Byer,	do.
Samuel Byer,	do.
Abraham Smith,	do.
Ulrick Hoover,	do.
Jacob Besler,	Philad'a Co.

Persons' names.	Of what place.
Jacob Hoover,	Lancaster Co.
John Kingry,	do.
Rudolph Behme,	Lancaster County.
Jacob Rhora,	do.
John Rhora,	do.
Andrew Ackre,	Bucks Co.
Philip Gavy,	do.
Peter Leman.	Lancaster Co.
John Meem,	Philad'a Co.
George Spingler,	do.
Henry Lebart,	Lancaster Co.
Martin Shultz,	do.
Christian Hoover,	do.
Hans Mussle,	do.

Certified by

JOHN KINSEY, *Ch. Just.*

[The foregoing is a true and perfect List taken from the original Certificate under the Hand of John Kinsey, Esq'r, remaining in my office.]

RICHARD PETERS, *Sec'ry.*

PHILADELPHIA, *4th October,* 1743.

Copy sent to London, on 4th Oct'r, 1743.

———

[And in like manner in April Term following, to wit: On the Tenth, Eleventh and Twelfth Days of April, 1744, at the said Supream Court, before the said Judges:]

Persons' names.	Of what place.	Time of taking the Sacrament.	
Philip Swickack,	Lancaster Co.,	23rd March,	1743–4
Geo. Thomas Sowder,	do.	8th April,	1744
John Wolfersparger,	do.	1st April,	1744
George Waterman,	do.	26th February,	1743
John Sheffer,	do.	25th March,	1744
Philip Shutz,	do.	26th February,	1743
Henry Saunder,	do.	6th April,	1744
Wyrick Pence,	do.	do.	
Jacob Hough,	do.	26th March,	1744
George Hough,	do.	do.	
Samuel Hough,	do.	do.	
Rudolph Draugh,	do.	25th March,	1744
George Swope,	do.	1st April,	1744
Christian Croll,	do.	18th March,	1743–4
Lodowick Willanger,	Philadelphia Co.,	25th March,	1744
George Croaner,	Bucks Co.,	do.	
John Richard,	Philadelphia Co.,	do.	

Persons' names.	Of what place.	Time of taking the Sacrament.	
Adam Simon Kuhn,	Lancaster Co.,	8th April,	1744
Baltzer Stever,	Bucks Co.,	25th March,	1744
Christian Stambaugh,	do.	do.	
Leonard Herman,	Philadelphia Co.,	1st April,	1744
Cronomus Hickman,	Lancaster Co.,	8th April,	1744
Valentine Unruw,	do.	2d April,	1744
John Ryall,	do.	do.	
Jacob Wilhelm,	do.	do.	
Elias Myer,	do.	25th March,	1744
Mathias Bettley,	do.	do.	
George Naffenberger,	do.	do.	
Peter Bernhard,	Philadelphia Co.,	1st April,	1744
Nicholas Carver,	Chester Co.,	5th April,	1744
John Cambree,	Philadelphia Co.,	1st April,	1744
Peter Gardner	Lancaster Co.,	11th April,	1744
George Ammond,	do.	do.	

. And at the same Court, the following Persons being Quakers or such who Conscientiously scruple to take an Oath, being also Foreigners, and having comply'd with the Terms required by the aforesaid Act of Parliament, Took and subscribed the Qualifications for them appointed by the same Act of Parliament, &ca., viz:

Persons' names.	Of what place.
Peter Bunn,	Philad'a Co.
John Frederick,	do.
John Miller,	Lancas'r Co.
Ulrick Lype,	do.
Henry Aberlee,	do.
Hans Shownower,	do.
John Hartman,	Philad'a Co.
Peter Good,	Lancaster Co.
John Faltz,	do.
Conrad Weiser,	do.
Oswald Hastadder,	do.
John Hastadder,	do.
Joseph Crell,	of Philadelphia City.

Certified by

JOHN KINSEY, *Ch. just.*

The foregoing is a true and perfect List, taken from the original Certificate under the Hand of John Kinsey, Esq'r, remaining in my office.

RICHARD PETERS, *Secr'y.*

PHILADELPHIA, *19th April*, 1744.

(Copy sent to the Secretary of the Lords of Trade, 5th Nov'r 1744. 2nd Copy sent in Nov'r, 1745.)

[And in like manner in September Term following, to wit: On the Twenty-fourth and Twenty-fifth Days of September, 1744, at the said Supream Court before the said Judges, in pursuance of the aforesaid Act of Parliament, the following Persons:]

Persons' names.	Of what place.	Time of taking the Sacrament.
John George Graff,	Lancaster Co.,	September 5th, 1744
John David Sickle,	Philadelphia Co.,	September 24th, 1744
Godfrey Brown,	Lancaster Co.,	Aug't 22d, 1744
John Philip De Bertholt,	Philad'a Co.,	September 24th, 1744
Andrew Wolf,	do.	September 16th, 1744
Henry Miller,	do.	Septem'r 24th, 1744
John Michael Heyter,	do.	do.

And at the same Court, the following Persons being Quakers, or such who conscientiously scruple to take an Oath, being also foreigners, and having complied with the Terms required by the aforesaid Act of Parliament, took and subscribed the Qualifications for them appointed by the same Act of Parliament, &c., viz:

Persons' names.	Of what place.
Christian Rodarmarle,	Philad'a County.
David Lodowick,	do.
Paul Rodarmarle,	do.
Jacob Hofman,	do.
Peter Loback,	do.
Leonard Hulster,	Lancaster Co.
Valentine Freeman,	do.
Andrew Strickler,	Lanc'r Co.
Andrew Elliott,	do.
John Johnston,	do.
Hans Garber,	do.
Michael Garber,	do.
Michael Brechth,	do.

Certified by

JOHN KINSEY, *Ch. just. Pennsylv.*

The foregoing is a true and perfect List, taken from the original Certificates under the Hand of John Kinsey, Esq'r, remaining in my office.

RICHARD PETERS, *Secr'y.*

PHILADELPHIA.

[Copy sent to London 5th Nov., 1744, Ex.—2nd Copy sent in Nov., 1745.]

[And in like manner, in April Term following, to wit: On the Tenth and Eleventh Days of April, 1745, at the said Supream Court, before the said Judges, in pursuance of the aforesaid Act of Parliament, the following Persons:

Persons' names.	Of what place.	Time of taking the Sacrament.
Jacob Heagy,	Lancaster Co.,	April 8th, 1745
Balthazar Sees,	do.	January 1st, 1744
David Kerger,	Philad'a Co.,	April 10th, 1745
Mathias Venrick,	Lancaster Co.,	Decem'r 25th, 1744

And at the same Court the fellow Persons being Quakers, or such who Conscientiously scruple to take an Oath, being also Foreigners, and having complied with the terms required by the aforesaid Act of Parliament, took and subscribed the Qualifications for them appointed by the same Act of Parliament, &ca., vizt:

Persons' names.	Of what place.
William Mye,	Philadelphia Co.
Urick Stoupher,	Lancaster Co.
Rudolph Salver,	Bucks Co.
Mathias Windle,	Philad'ia Co.
Benjamin Boucher,	Lancaster Co.
Casper Creesermer,	Philadelphia Co.
George Riter,	do.
Nicholas Eyes,	do.

RICHARD PETERS.

The foregoing is a true and perfect List, taken from the original Certificate under the Hand of John Kensy, Esq'r, remaining in my office.

RICHARD PETERS, *Sec'y.*

PHILADELPHIA, 10*th Novem'r,* 1745.
Copy sent to London 11th Nov. 1745.

———

[And in like manner in September Term following, to wit: On the Twenty-fourth day of September, 1745, at the said Supream Court, before the said Judges in pursuance of the aforesaid Act of Parliament, the following Persons:]

Persons' names.	Of what county.
Abraham Hartrampff,	Philadelphia.
George Wigner,	do.
Abraham Wigner,	do.
Melchoir Mayster,	do.
George Hoffman,	do.
Chistopher Kribeld,	do.
George Reinwalt,	do.

Persons' names.	Of what county.
Christopher Seibb,	Philadelphia.
Christopher Hibner,	do.
David Hibner,	do.
Michael Schairer,	Lancaster.
Jonens Joner,	do.
Christian Gemelin,	Philadelphia.
Philip Shaffer,	Lancaster.
Michael Brooks,	do.
David Shubert,	Philadelphia.
Jacob Beidleman,	Bucks.

Certify'd by

JOHN KINSEY, Ch. just.

The foregoing is a true and perfect List, taken from the original Certificate under the Hand of John Kinsey, Esqr., remaining in my office.

RICHARD PETERS.

PHILADELPHIA, 11th Novem'r, 1745.

30 May, 1746. Sent to London.

[And in like manner, in April Term following, to wit: On the Tenth and eleventh days of April, 1746, At the said Supream Court, before the said Judges, in pursuance of the aforesaid Act of Parliament, the following Persons:]

Persons' names.	Of what place.	Time of taking the Sacrament.	
Valentine Urich,	Lancaster County,	February 2nd,	1745
Martin Kalder,	do.	do.	
John Lobwick Seiple,	Philadelphia City,	April 4th,	1746
Jacob Maag,	do.	do.	
Jacob Weine,	do.	do.	
Michael Lutz,	Bucks County,	February 2nd,	1745
George Ruch,	do.	do.	
Michael Ruch,	do.	do.	
John Justice Jacob Bergestock, Clerk,	do.	do.	

And at the same Court the following Persons, being Quakers, or such who conscientiously scruple to take an oath, being also foreigners and having complied with * * * required by the aforesaid Act of Parliament, took and subscribed the Qualifications for them appointed by the same Act of Parliament, &c., viz:

Persons' names.	Of what county.
Jacob Reiser,	Lancaster.
John Keider,	Philadelphia.
John Shlichter,	Philadelphia.

Persons' names.	Of what county.
Abraham Rife,	Philadelphia.
Jacob Ruch,	Philadelphia.
Certify'd by	

JOHN KINSEY,
Ch. Just. of the Province of Pennsylv'a.

The foregoing is a true and perfect List, taken from the original Certificate, under the Hand of John Kinsey, Esqr., remaining in my office.

RICHARD PETERS, *Sec'y.*

PHILADELPHIA, 30*th May,* 1746.
Sent Duplicate in Aug., 1748.

[And in like manner, in September Term following, to wit: On the twenty-fourth day of September, 1746, at the said Supream Court, before the said Judges, in pursuance of the aforesaid Act of Parliament, the following Persons:]

Persons' names.	Of what place.	Time of taking the Sacrament.	
Johannes Rudolph,	Philadelphia Co.,	July 27th,	1746
George Horne,	do.	September 14th,	1746
Leonard Nutz,	Lancaster County,	September 21st,	1746
Simon Shirman,	do.	September 21st,	1746
Johannes Mayer,	do.	August 31st,	1746
Johannes Haberling,	do.	September 14,	1746

And at the same Court the following Persons, being Quakers, or such who conscientiously scruple to take an Oath, being also Foreigners, and having complied with the Terms required by the aforesaid Act of Parliament, Took and subscribed the Qualifications for them appointed by the same act of Parliament, &c., viz:

Persons' names.	Of what place.
Michael Mesinger,	Philadelphia County.
Jacob Meily,	Lancaster County.
Peter Folk,	do.
John Snievly,	Lancaster County.
Henry Heilman,	Philadelphia Co.
Valentine Heyser,	Philadelphia Co.
Certified by	

JOHN KINSEY,
Chief Justice of the Province of Pennsylvania.

The foregoing is a true and perfect List taken from the original certificate, under the Hand of John Kinsey, Esq'r, remaining in my office.

RICHARD PETERS.

PHILADELPHIA, 30*th May,* 1747.
Sent Duplicate in Aug., 1748.

[And in like manner in April Term following, to wit: On the tenth, eleventh, thirteenth and fourteenth days of April, 1747, at the said Supream Court, before the said Judges, in pursuance of the aforesaid Act of Parliament, the following Persons, viz:]

Persons' names.	Of what place.	Time of taking the Sacrament.	
Johann Daniel Bouton,	Philadelphia City,	February 1st,	1746
Elias Stricker,	Philadelphia Co.,	do.	
John Stricker,	Philadelphia City,	do.	
Michael Reis,	Lancaster County,	March 8th,	1746
Johannes Wolfert,	do.	do.	
Christian Myer,	do.	do.	
George Brosius,	do.	do.	
Jacob Hoffman,	do.	do.	
Adam Morgan,	Philadelphia Co.,	April 5th,	1747
George Kern,	do.	March 30th,	1747
Rev. M. Tobias Wage-nar,	do.	March 25th,	1747
George Kocker,	do.	January 18,	1746
John Christopher Cun,	do.	March 28.	1747
Leonard Reiber,	do.	do.	
Philip Mann,	do.	do.	
John Philip Dold,	Philadelphia Co.,	April 5th,	1747
Jacob Muller,	do.	do.	
Godfried Harlacher,	Philadelphia Co.,	April 5th,	1747
George Dannehaucr,	do.	do.	
Adam Hinton,	do.	do.	
Paul Geisel,	do	April 12th,	1747
Michael Ege,	do.	do.	
Christopher Loist,	do.	March 25th,	1747

And at the same Court, Moses Heyman, of Philadelphia County, a Jew, and the other following Persons being Quakers or such who Conscientiously scruple to take an Oath, being also Foreigners, and having complied with the terms required by the aforesaid Act of Parliament. Took and subscribed the Qualifications for them appointed by the same Act of Parlia ment, &ca., viz:

Persons' names.	Of what place.
Ludwig Plum,	Philadelphia County.
Peter Prett,	Lancaster County.
Nicholas Cron,	Philadelphia Co.
Daniel Womelsdorff,	do.
Elias Beidleman,	Bucks Co.
Christopher Croffern,	Lancaster Co.
John Drout,	Philadelphia Co.
Valentine Lier,	Lancaster Co.

Persons' names.	*Of what place.*
Herick Rotter,	Bucks Co.
Johannes Eigenter,	Bucks Co.
Dominicus Gassner,	Philadelphia Co.
Conrad Weigner,	do.
Nicholas Kroft,	do.
John Housom,	Lancaster Co.

Certified by

JOHN KINSEY, *Chief Just.,*
of the Province of Pennsylvania.

The foregoing is a true and perfect List, taken from the original Certificate, under the Hand of John Kinsey, Esqr., remaining in my office.

RICHARD PETERS.

PHILADELPHIA, 30*th May,* 1747.

The Lords of Trade have received all certificates to this time.

RICHARD PETERS.

Sent Duplicates in Aug't, 1748.

———

[And in like manner, in September Term following, to wit: On the Twenty-fifth day of September, in the year of our Lord 1747, at the said Supream Court, before the said Judges, in pursuance of the aforesaid Act of Parliament, The following Persons, viz:]

Persons' names.	*Of what place*	*Time of taking the Sacrament.*	
Jacob Vonderwiyt,	Philadelphia Co.,	June 29th,	1747
Peter Spycher,	do.	August 23rd,	1747
John George Crysman,	do.	do.	
George Poger,	do.	do.	
Peter Holtzetter.	do.	do.	

And at the same Court the following Persons, being Quakers, or such who Conscientiously scruple to take an Oath, being also Foreigners & having complied with the Terms required by the aforesaid Act of Parliament, Took and subscribed the Qualifications for them appointed by the same Act of Parliament, &c., viz:

Persons' names.	*Of what place.*
Christopher Highmager,	Bucks County.
Christian Sensenig,	Lancaster Co.
Adam Stout,	Philadelphia Co.
Henrick Wyerman,	Bucks County.
John Lob,	do.
Christian Souder,	Philadelphia Co.

Certified by

JOHN KINSEY.

The foregoing is a true and perfect List, taken from the original Certificate, under the Hand of John Kinsey, Esqr., remaining in my office.

RICHARD PETERS.

PHILADELPHIA, 30*th May*, 1748.
Copy sent per Capt. Smyter.

[And in like manner, in April Term following, to wit: On the thirteenth and fifteenth days of April, 1748, at the said Supream Court, before the said Judges, in pursuance of the aforesaid Act of Parliament, the following Persons, viz:

Persons' names.	Of what place.	Time of taking the Sacrament.	
Jacob Nuss,	Philadelphia County,	April 9th,	1748
George Mill,	do. County,	April 10,	1748
Peter Somy,	Lancaster County,	do.	
Johannes Lehmenn,	Philadelphia County,	do.	
George Emann,	do.	do.	
Michael Yoachum,	do.	do.	
Henry Ramsaur,	do.	do.	
George Noll,	Lancaster County,	April 11th,	1748
Jacob Hauck,	Bucks County,	April 3rd,	1748
Philip Balshazar Croesman,	Philadelphia County,	March 13th,	1747
Adam Clampferr,	Philadelphia City,	April 10th,	1748
William Clampferr,	do.	do.	
Mathias Lambert,	Lancaster County,	do.	
Wendal Neft,	Philadelphia County,	do.	
Michael Durr,	Philadelphia City,	do.	

And at the same Court Christopher Krause, of Philadelphia County, who conscientiously scruples to take an Oath, being a Foreigner, and having complied with the terms required by the aforesaid Act of Parliament, Took and subscribed the Qualifications for them appointed by the same Act of Parliament, &ca.

The foregoing is a true and perfect List, taken from the original Certificate, under the Hand of John Kinsey, Esqr., remaining in my office.

RICHARD PETERS, *Secr'y.*

PHILADELPHIA, 30*th May*, 1748.
(Copy sent per Capt. Smyter.)

[And in like manner, in September term following, to wit: On the twenty-sixth day of September, 1748, at the said Supream Court, before the said Judges, in pursuance of the aforesaid Act of Parliament, the following persons, viz:

Persons' names.	Of what place.	Time of taking the Sacrament.
Michael Becker,	Philadelphia County, lives in the Northern Liberties of the City of Philadelphia,	September 18th, 174
Anthony Newhouse,	Philadelphia County,	The same day.
Johannes Ebler,	Lancaster County,	July 22d, 174
Johan Peter Traxel,	Bucks County,	September 5th, 174
Magdalen Anspachen, wife of Peter Anspächen,	Lancaster County,	July 22d, 174
Jacob Geari,	Philadelphia County,	September 4th, 174
Casper Holtzhousen.	Bucks County,	September 5th, 174
Margaret Reis, wife of Michael Reis,	Lancaster County,	September 22d, 174
Anna Maria Naefen, wife of Michael Naefen,	Lancaster County,	July 22d, 174
Andrew Miller,	Lancaster County,	September 22d, 174

And at the same Court the following persons, being Quakers
or such who conscientiously scruple to take an oath, being also
foreigners & having complied with the Terms required by the
aforesaid act of Parliament, took and subscribed the Qualifications for them appointed by the same act of Parliament
&ca.,

Persons' names.	Of what place.
Melchior Hartramff,	Philadelphia County.
Jacob Yoner,	Lancaster County.
John Bucks,	do.

Certified by Thomas Græme, the chief Justice being deceased
The foregoing is a true and perfect List taken from the origna
certificate, under the Hand of Thomas Græme, Esqr., remaining in my office.

RICHARD PETERS, Secr'y.

Philadelphia, 1st June, 1749.

(Transmitted by the Caroline, Capt. Meshard.)

———

[And in like manner, in April Term following, to wit: On the
eleventh day of April, 1749, at the said Supream Court, before
the said Judges, in Pursuance of the aforesaid Act of Parliament
the following Persons, viz:]

Persons' names.	Of what place.	Time of taking the Sacrament.	
Michael Nees,	Lancaster Co.,	25th March,	1749
Hendrick Heilig,	Philadelphia Co.,	26th March,	1749
Henry Shellenberg,	Philadelphia Co.,	25th March,	1749
William Labaer,	Bucks County,	25th March,	1749
Conrad Timberman,	Philadelphia Co.,	18th March,	1749
Anna Dorethea Heiz,	Bucks County,	26th March,	1749
Mathias Reel,	do.	25th March,	1749
Daniel Hister,	Philadelphia Co.,	25th March,	1749
Michael Hillegas,	do.	26th March,	1749
George Shive,	do.	25th March,	1749
Peter Scholl,	Bucks County,	do.	
Michael Reitter,	Philadelphia Co.,	do.	
Lawrence Dehr,	do.	do.	
Andrew Boyer,	do.	do.	
Abraham Faust,	Bucks County,	do.	
Henrick Young,	Philadelphia Co.,	do.	
Nicholas Raush,	do.	do.	
John Gaufres,	do.	do.	
Adam Miller,	Philadelphia Co.,	25th March,	1749
John George Rott,	Bucks County,	do.	
Michael Small,	Lancaster County,	do.	
John Jacob Fox,	Philadelphia Co.,	31st March,	1749
John Widman,	Lancaster Co.,	25th March,	1749
Conrad Schneider,	Philadelphia Co.,	do.	
Nicholas Icks,	do.	26th March,	1749
John Stone,	Lancaster Co.,	25th March,	1749
Adam Moser,	do.	do.	
David Stripe,	do.	do.	

And at the same Court, the following Persons being Quakers or such who conscientiously scruple to take an Oath, being also Foreigners, and having complied with the terms required by the aforesaid Act of Parliament, took and subscribed the Qualifications for them appointed by the same Act of Parliament, &ca.

Persons' names.	Of what place.
Felix Brunner,	Bucks County,
Michael Keller,	do.
Jacob Dubes,	do.
John Huber	do.
Christian Willower,	do.
Jacob Wetzel,	do.
Peter Etter,	Philadelphia County.
Jacob Frank,	do.

21—VOL. II.

Persons' names.	Of what place.
Daniel Etter,	Philadelphia County.
Thomas Hail,	do.
Andrew Godshall,	do.
John Grout,	do.
Henry Bowman,	Lancaster County.
Casper Sherick,	do.

Certified by Thomas Græme, the Chief Justice being deceasec

The foregoing is a true and perfect List, taken from the orig nal Certificate under the Hand of Thomas Græme, Esqr., r maining in my office.

RICHARD PETERS, *Sec'ry.*

PHILADELPHIA, 1st *June,* 1749.

(Transmitted to the board of Trade in the Carolina, Cap' Mishard.)

———

[And in like manner in September Term following, to wit: O the Twenty-fifth & twenty-sixth Days of September, and fourt day of October, 1749, at the same Supream Court before the sai Judges, in pursuance of the aforesaid act of Parliament, th following Persons:]

Persons' names.	Of what place	Sacrament, when taken.
Valentine Stober,	Lancaster County,	August 27th, 174
Henry Mots,	do.	September 17th, 174
Peter Baker,	do.	August 27th, 174
Solomon Libkep,	Bucks County,	September 17th, 174
John Dethrick Held,	Philadelphia Co.,	August 6th, 174
John Grose,	do.	do.
John William Fisher,	Lancaster County,	September 30th, 174
Philip Filchmir,	do.	do.
Francis Creek,	do.	do.
Christopher Orish,	do.	September 17th, 174
Conrad Frick,	Philadelphia Co.,	September 3d, 174
John Sigismund Hane- ly,	Lancaster County,	September 19, 174
Andrew Creutzer,	do.	September 30th, 174
Michael Miller,	do.	do.
Michael Axer,	do.	do.
Lodowick Cornman,	do.	do.
Godfret Reorher,	do.	do.
Adam Linn,	York County,	August 27th, 174

Joseph Simon, of the County & Borough of Lancaster, *A Jeu*

The person last mentioned, Joseph Simon, being a Jew, wa qualified and subscribed the Declaration, &ca., according t the directions of the act of the thirteenth of King George th

Second aforementioned, and at the same Court the following persons, being Quakers, or such who conscientiously scruple to take an Oath, being also Foreigners, and having complied with the terms required by the aforesaid act of Parliament, took and subscribed the Qualifications for them appointed by the same act of Parliament, &ca. :

Persons' names.	Of what place.
John Christopher Heebner,	Philadelphia County.
Melchior Creeble,	do.
Christopher Wagner,	do.
Casper Seibt,	do.
Christopher Hoffman,	do.

Certified by Thomas Græme, the Chief Justice being deceased.

The foregoing is a true and perfect List, taken from the original certificate, under the Hand of Thomas Græme, Esqr., remaining in my office.

RICHARD PETERS, *Secr'y.*

PHILADELPHIA, *1st June*, 1750.

(Transmitted by the Carolina, Capt. Mesherd.)

———

[And in like manner, in April Term following, to wit: On the twelfth day of April, 1750, at the said supream Court, before the said Judges, in pursuance of the aforesaid act of Parliament, the following persons, viz. :

Persons' names.	Of what place.	Sacrament, when taken.	
Andrew Miller,	Philadelphia Co.,	April the 8,	1750
Dietheric Ramsaur,	do.	March the 25th,	1750
Adam Wartham.	do.	April the 8th,	1750

And at the same Court the following persons, being Quakers, or such who conscientiously scruple to take an oath, being also Foreigners, and having complied with the Terms required by the aforesaid act of Parliament, took and subscribed the Qualifications for them appointed by the same act of Parliament, &ca. :

Persons' names.	Of what place.
Adam Drullinger,	Bucks County.
Jacob Brua,	Lancaster County.
John Stoner,	Chester County.
Martin Bechtel,	Philad'a County.
Christian Blim,	do.
Peter Engle,	Chester County.
Christian Croup,	Lancaster County.
Christian Perry,	Chester County.
Andrew Heit,	do.
Roderick Smith,	do.

Persons' names.	Of what place,
Jacob Weiss,	Of Philadelphia Count & City, he being one (the people called the M(ravian Brethren, receiv ed the sacrament amon them in the 1st Apri 1750, as ℔ certificate.
Joseph Sherrick,	Lancaster County.
Michael Swoope,	York County.
Jacob Shantz,	Philad'a County.
Henry Bear,	Chester County.

And at a Court of Oyer and Terminer & General Gaol D(livery, held at Lancaster, for the County of Lancaster, on th second day of May, 1750, before the Justices aforesaid, Benjami Widmer, who conscientiously scruples to take an Oath, bein a Foreigner, took the affirmations & made the Declarations, an subscribed the same according to the directions of the Act (Parliament aforesaid,

Certified by

THOMAS GRÆME,

(the Chief Justice being deceased.)

The foregoing is a true & perfect List taken from the origina Certificate, under the Hand of Thomas Græme, Esq'r, remainin in my office.

RICHARD PETERS, Sec'ry.

PHILADELPHIA, 1st June, 1750.

(Sent by the Carolina, Capt. Meshard.)

[And in like manner in September Term following, to wit On the twenty-fifth day of September, 1750, at the said Suprear Court, before William Allen, Lawrence Growdon and Cale Cowpland, Esquires, Judges of the said Court, in pursuanc of the aforesaid Act of Parliament, the following Persons, viz

Persons' names.	Of what place.	Sacrament, when taken	
Peter Pener	Philad'a County,	September 9th,	17£
Frederick Wambold,	do.	August 26th,	17£
George Winter,	do.	August 5th,	17£
Adam Rifel,	do.	September 16th,	17£
Michael Hauk,	do.	July 3rd,	17£
Philip Shreiner,	Lancaster County,	September 21st,	175
Leonard Billmyer,	do.	September 21,	175
John Valentine Shreiner,	do.	August 18th,	17£
Jacob Billmyer,	York County,	September 2d,	175
Jacob Fackler,	do.	September 2,	175

Persons' names.	Of what place	Sacrament, when taken.	
Herman Bott,	York County,	September 2,	1750
Christopher Trencle,	Lancaster County,	August 5,	1750
Nicholas Havener,	do.	September 16,	1750
Peter Gebhart,	do.	September 16,	1750

And at the same Court the following Persons being Quakers, or such who conscientiously scruple to take an oath, being also Foreigners, and having complied with the Terms required by the aforesaid Act of Parliament, took and subscribed the Qualifications for them appointed by the same act of Parliament, &ca. :

Persons' names	Of what place.
David Nitschman,	Bucks County. A Mori-

vian took sacrament August 27th, 1751, as certified by the B'p of the United Brethren at Bethlehem.

Ruthol Lap,	Philadelphia County.
Melchior Heavenor,	Philadelphia County.
John Christy,	Lancaster County.
John Furry,	Lancaster County.
Ulrich Shulleberg,	do.
Henry Strickler,	do.
Bastian Haupt,	Philad'a County.
Henry Snider,	Lancaster County.

Certified by

WILLIAM ALLEN, Esqr.,
Chief Justice.

The foregoing is a true and perfect List, taken from the original Certificate under the Hand of William Allen, Esquire, remaining in my office.

RICHARD PETERS.

Philadelphia, *1st July,* 1751.

(Transmitted to the Board of Trade by Capt. Montpelier, 7th July, 1753.)

[And in like manner in April Term following, to wit: On the eleventh day of April, 1751, at the said Supream Court, before the said Judges, in pursuance of the aforesaid Act of Parliament, the following Persons, viz:]

Persons' names.	Of what place.	Sacrament, when taken.	
Stephen Conrad,	Lancaster County,	April 7th,	1751
John George Kehl,	do.	April 7,	1751
Maria Ursula Kelm,	do.	April 7,	1751
Mathias Smith,	do.	April 7,	1751
Nicholas Bittell,	Philad'a County,	April 7,	1751
George Klepinger,	do.	April 7,	1751

Persons' names.	Of what place.	Sacrament, when taken	
Jonas Kohler,	Philad'a County,	April 7,	1751
Jacob Reidy,	do.	April 7,	1751
Henry Reid,	do.	April 7,	1751
John Fisher,	do.	April 7,	1751
Bernard Lowman,	York County,	March 24,	1750
Joseph Solomon.	Lancaster County,	(A Jew, sworn on	
the Old Testam't only.)			
Bern'rd Laubersweiler,	Philad'a County,	April 8,	1751
Bernard Kolsinger,	York County,	March 24,	1750
Martin Bower,	do.	March 24,	1750
Conrad Shutz,	Philad'a County,	April 7,	1751
Henry Shutz,	do.	April 7,	1751
Jacob Whightman,	do.	April 7,	1751
Conrad Keehmle,	do.	April 10,	1751
Mathias Bush.	do.	(A Jew, sworn on the Old Tes't	
only.)			
Adam Weber,	do.	April 7,	1751
Charles Ewald,	do.	April 7,	1751
John Frederick Vigera,	do.	April 7,	1751
Jacob Roar.	Bucks County,	April 7,	1751

And at the same Court, the following Persons being Quakers, or such who Conscientiously scruple to take an Oath, being also Foreigners, and having complied with the Terms, required by the aforesaid Act of Parliament, took and subscribed the Qualifications for them appointed by the same Act of Parliament, &ca., vizt:

Persons' names.	Of what place.
Leonard Sing,	Philadelphia County,
Urich Peninger,	do.
John Roistrock.	Bucks County,
Jacob Stout,	do.
Christian Koplin,	Philadelphia County.
Martin Boeler, a Moravian,	Lancaster County.

[Took the sacrament some weeks before the 8th day of April, 1751, the day of the date of the certificate of the Reverend Mr. Christian Rauch as tis expressed in the said certificate.]

Michael Hoversticht,	Lancaster County.
Jacob Rubley,	do.
Philip Kerker,	Philad'a County.
George Slipplear,	Lancaster County.
William Young,	Philadelphia County.

Certified by   WILLIAM ALLEN, Esqr.,
Chief Justice.

The foregoing is a true and perfect List, taken from the original Certificate under the Hand of William Allen, Esquire, remaining in my office.

RICHARD PETERS.

PHILADELPHIA, 1st *June*, 1751.

(Transmitted to the board of Trade by Capt. Montpelier, 7th July, 1753.)

———

[And in like manner, in September Term following, to wit: On the Twenty-fifth day of September, 1751, at the said Supream Court, before the said Judges, in pursuance of the aforesaid Act of Parliament, the following Persons:]

Persons' names.	Of what place.	Sacrament, when taken.		
Philip Cunius,	Philad'a County,	22d	September,	1751
Daniel Muller,	Bucks County,	20	September,	1751
George Pry,	Philad'a County,	20	September,	1751
George Leidick,	do.	22	September,	1751
John Nicholas Seydel,	do.	1	September,	1751
Eva Barbara Holstein,	Lancaster County,	15	September,	1751
Andrew Groff,	do.	15	September,	1751
Martin Kapp,	do.	15	September,	1751
Eva Margaretta Kapp,	do.	15	September,	1751
Christian Muller,	do.	15	September,	1751
Eva Maria Muller,	do.	15	September,	1751
George Emmert,	do.	15	September,	1751
Eva Maria Emmert,	do.	15	September,	1751
Peter Werner,	do.	15	September,	1751
Philip Hautz,	do.	22	September,	1751
Philip Lawrence Hautz,	do.	22	September,	1751
John Sieble,	do.	22	September,	1751
Daniel Houy,	do.	14	September,	1751
George Larow,	Chester County,	18	August,	1751
Jonas Larow,	Lancaster County,	19	July,	1751
Peter Pisel,	Philad'a County,	15	September,	1751
George Slacker,	do.	22	September,	1751
George Lechner,	Lancaster County,	15	September,	1751
George Dollinger,	do.	15	September,	1751
Jacob Katterman,	do.	15	September,	1751
Francis Wenery,	do.	22	September,	1751
Peter Laucks,	do.	22	September,	1751
John Trautman,	do.	22	September,	1751
John Imel,	do.	15	September,	1751
Simon Carll,	do.	15	September,	1751
George Hoffman,	Bucks county,	3	September,	1751
Jacob Wart,	do.	22	September,	1751

Persons' names.	Of what place.		Sacrament, when taken.	
John George Lechner,	Lancaster County,	15	September,	1751
Michael Ebert,	York County,	1	September,	1751
Martin Ebert,	do.	1	September,	1751
Balthazar Knoertzer,	do.	1	September,	1751
Martin Watz,	Lancaster County,	1	September,	1751
Ulrich Nesley,	Philad'a County,	3	August,	1741
John Peter Speiht,	do.	22	September,	1751
Henry Keller,	Bucks County,	24	September,	1751

And at the same Court, the following Persons being Quakers, or such who Conscientiously scruple to take an oath, being also Foreigners, and having complied with the Terms required by the aforesaid Act of Parliament, took and subscribed the Qualifications for them appointed by the same Act of Parliament, &c., viz:

Persons' names.	Of what place.
Valentine Stickle,	Philadelphia County.
Conrad Bop,	do.
George Woolford,	Lancaster County.
Peter Simerman,	do.
Jacob Machlen,	Philadelphia County.
Jeremiah Jackle,	Philadelphia County.
George Graff,	Lancaster County.
Killean Wies,	Philad'a County.
Melchior Meng,	Philad'a County.

Certified by

WILLIAM ALLEN, Esquire, *Chief Justice.*

The foregoing is a true and perfect List, taken from the original Certificate under the Hand of William Allen, Esqr., remaining in my office.

RICHARD PETERS.

PHILADELPHIA.

(Transmitted to the Board of Trade by Capt. Montpelier, 7 July, 1753.)

[And in like manner, in April Term following, to wit: On the eleventh day of April, 1752, at the said Supream Court, before the said Judges, in Pursuance of the aforesaid Act of Parliament, the following Persons:]

Persons' names.	Of what place.	Sacrament, when taken.	
Martin Eisenhaver,	Lancaster County,	29th March,	1752
Peter Eisenhaver,	do.	29 March.	1752
Elizabeth Eisenhaver,	do.	29 March	1752
John George Grof,	do.	4 April,	1752
Jeremiah Tracsler,	Bucks County,	29 March,	1752

Persons' names	Of what place.	Sacrament, when taken.	
Henry Oal,	Bucks County,	29 March,	1752
Elias Bonder,	do.	29 March,	1752
John Short,	do.	29 March,	1752
Peter Woodring,	do.	29 March,	1752
Henry Walter,	Lancaster County,	29 March,	1752
William Hauker,	do.	29 March,	1752
Thomas Dormer,	Philadelphia City,	29 March,	1752

And at the same Court the following Persons being Quakers, or such who conscientiously scruple to take an oath, being also Foreigners, and having complied with the terms required by the aforesaid act of Parliament, took and subscribed the Qualifications for them appointed by the same act of Parliament, &ca :

Persons' names.	Of what place.
Cornelius Lane,	Lancaster County.
Peter Lane,	do.
Bolser Spangler,	York County.
Henry Everli,	Lancaster County.
John Adam Schaws,	Philadelphia County.
Certified by	

WILLIAM ALLEN, Esquire, *Chief Justice.*

The foregoing is a true and perfect List, taken from the original Certificate, under the Hand of William Allen, Esq'r, remaining in my office.

RICHARD PETERS.

PHILADELPHIA.

(Transmitted to the Board of Trade By Capt. Montpelier, 7 July, 1753.)

—

[And in like manner in September Term ·following, to wit : On the Twenty-fifth day of September, 1752, at the said Supream Court, before the said Judges, in pursuance of the aforesaid act of Parliament, the following persons :]

Persons' names.	Of what place.	Sacrament, when taken.	
Jacob Folmar,	Berks County,	August	16, 1752
Frederick Hertsog,	Philad'a County,	September	20, 1752
Solomon Heim Bonn,	Philad'a City,	} Jews, sworn on the	
Michael Israel,	do.	} Old Testament only.	

And at the same Court, the following Persons being Quakers, or such who conscientiously scruple to take an Oath, being also Foreigners, and having complied with the Terms required by the aforesaid Act of Parliament, took and subscribed the Qualifications for them appointed by the same Act of Parliament, &c., viz:

Persons' names.	*Of what place.*
George Nicholas Mayer, ·	Philadelphia City.
Andrew Wint,	Northampton County.
Paul Anthony,	Philadelphia County.
Frederick Baker,	Philadelphia City.

Certified by

WILLIAM ALLEN, Esquire,
Chief Justice.

The foregoing is a true and perfect List, taken from the original Certificate under the Hand of William Allen, Esquire, remaining in my office.

RICHARD PETERS.

Philadelphia.

(Transmitted to the Board of Trade by Capt. Budden, 20th August, 1753.)

———

[And in like manner, in April Term following, to wit: On the Tenth day of April, 1753, at the said Supream Court, before the said judges, in Pursuance of the aforesaid act of Parliament, the following persons:]

Persons' names.	*Of what place.*	*Sacrament, when taken.*
Peter Smidt,	Lancaster County, April,	8, 1753
Michael Hoobley,	Lancaster County, February, 14,	1753
Peter Backer,	Philadelphia Co., April, 8,	1753

And at the same Court the following Persons being Quakers, or such who conscientiously scruple to take an oath, being also Foreigners, and having complied with the Terms required by the aforesaid act of Parliament, took and subscribed the Qualifications for them appointed by the same act of Parliament, &c:

Persons' names.	*Of what place.*
Lewis Clots,	Northampton County.
Peter Miller, Jun'r,	Philadelphia City.
Adam Redd,	York County.
John Eggman,	Lancaster County.
Marcus Forney,	York County.
Conrad Price,	Berks County.
Henry Konn,	York County.
Christian Hoober,	Lancaster County.
John Shultz,	York County.
Leonard Fessler,	Lancaster County.
George Werfield,	Lancaster County.
Melchior Werfield,	Lancaster County.
Jacob Ehrenhart,	Northampton County.
John Knauss,	Northampton County.
Adam Shuder,	do.

Persons' names.	Of what place.
Martin Stutzman,	Berks Co.
Peter Sites,	Lancaster County.
Francis Rutter,	Berks Co.
George Rutter,	do.
Rudolph Heckeler,	do.
Sebast'n Henry Knauss,	Northampton Co.
John Wagner,	Berks Co.
John Franckleberger,	York Co.
Anthony Deshler,	Philad'a City.
Frederick Romig,	North'n Co.
Conrad Kearsner,	Berks Co.

Certified by

WILLIAM ALLEN, Esquire, *Chief Justice.*

The foregoing is a true and perfect List taken from the original Certificate, under the Hand of William Allen, Esq'r, remaining in my office.

RICHARD PETERS.

(Transmitted to the Board of Trade by Capt. Budden, 20th August, 1753.)

———

[And in like manner in September Term following, to wit: On the Twenty-fourth day of September, 1753, at the said Supream Court, before the said Judges in pursuance of the aforesaid Act of Parliament, the following Persons:]

Persons' names.	Of what place.	Sacrament, when taken.	
George Esterly,	Philadelphia County,	the 16 September,	1753
Martin Bumbarger,	Lancaster County,	the 26 August,	1753
Jacob Orndt,	Bucks County,	the 9 September,	1753
Henry Bumberger,	Bucks County,	the 9 September,	1753
John Martin,	Philadelphia County,	the 20 August,	1753
Peter Geerhart,	Philadelphia County,	the 9 September,	1753
Jacob Lydie,	Philadelphia County,	the 16 September,	1753
Bernard Kountzer,	Philadelphia County,	the 16 September,	1753
Benjamin Spyker,	Lancaster County,	the 26 August,	1753
Henry Toopes,	Lancaster County,	the 16 September,	1753
Henry Geyer,	Philadelphia County,	the 22 September,	1753
Michael Dodererer,	Berks County,	the 22 September,	1753
Michael Fortnee,	Lancaster County,	the 22 September,	1753
George Metzger,	Lancaster County,	the 2 September,	1753
Abraham Hoobler,	Lancaster County,	the 16 September,	1753

Persons' names.	Of what place.	Sacrament, when taken.	
Jacob Eicholtz,	Lancaster County,	the 2 September,	1753
John Michael By-erly,	Lancaster County.	the 2 September,	1753
Ludwick Lau-man,	Lancaster County,	the 2 September,	1753
Michael Gross,	Lancaster County,	the 19 September,	1753
Valentine Krug,	Lancaster County,	the 2 September,	1753
John Barr,	Lancaster County,	the 26 August,	1753

And at the same Court, the following Persons being Quakers or such who conscientiously scruple to take an oath, being also Foreigners, and having complied with the Terms required by the aforesaid Act of Parliament, Took and subscribed the Qualifications for them appointed by the Act of Parliament, &ca. :

Persons' names.	Of what place.
Benedict Estleman,	Lancaster County.
Michael Hess,	Lancaster County.
Johannes Thomas,	Lancaster County.
Jacob Markley,	Philadelphia Co.
Jacob Roff,	City of Philadelphia.
Garrard Brenor,	Lancaster County.
Michael Shaver,	Berks County.
Frederick Shaver	Berks County.
John Beeser,	Berks County.
Peter Shaver,	Berks County.
John Yerb,	Lancaster County.
Melker Wagoner,	Philadelphia Co.
Daniel Kepotz,	Lancaster County,
Wendall Whole,	Lancaster County.
John Bowman,	Lancaster County.
Jacob Yerb,	Lancaster C'y.
Isaac Whole,	Lancaster C'y.

Certified by

WILLIAM ALLEN, Esquire, *Chief Justice.*

The foregoing is a true and perfect List from the original Certificate, under the Hand of William Allen, Esquire, remaining in my office.

RICHARD PETERS.

[And in like manner, in April Term following, to wit: On the tenth day of April, 1754, at the said Supream Court, before the said Judges, in pursuance of the aforesaid Act of Parliament, the following Persons, viz:]

Persons' names.	Of what place.	Sacrament, when taken.	
Valentine Nungas-ser,	Philadelphia County,	31st March,	1754
Charles Swartz,	do.	do.	

Persons' names,	Of what place.	Sacrament, when taken.	
Daniel Kokert,	Northampton County,	the 7th April,	1754
Michael Wilhelm.	do.	the 10th April,	1754
Jacob Miller,	Berks County,	do.	
Jacob Deck,	Northampton County,	the 7th April,	1754
Casper Ritter,	do.	the 10th of April,	1754
Jacob Pfister,	Philadelphia County,	the 14th April,	1754
Martin Gatler,	do.	the 14th do.	
Mathias Cline,	do.	do.	
George Jacob Young,	do.	do.	
Johannes Neglee,	do.	do.	
Jacob Whitman,	do.	do.	
John Cubber,	do.	do.	
Christopher Gatler,	do.	do.	
George Hoffman,	do.	do.	
Jacob Swenke,	do.	do.	
Henry Maag,	do.	do.	

And at the same Court, the following persons being Quakers, or such who conscientiously scruple to take an oath, being also foreigners, and having complied with the Terms required by the aforesaid Act of Parliament, took and subscribed the Qualifications for them appointed by the same Act of Parliament, &ca. :

Persons' names.	Of what place.
Andrew Boyer,	Berks County.
John Sarver,	do.
Ernast Sigomond Seydle,	do.
David Ely,	do.
Philip Epright,	Lancaster County.
Ulrick Stoy,	Berks County.
Michael Daiser,	Lancaster County.
Leonard Stone,	do.
Leonard Miller,	do.
Jacob Kern,	Berks County.
John Gonkle,	Lancaster County.
Christian Neegle,	Northampt'n Co.
Daniel Remick,	do.

Certified by

WILLIAM ALLEN, Esquire, *Chief Justice.*

The foregoing is a true and perfect list from the original certificate under the Hand of William Allen, Esq'r, remain'g in my office.

RICHARD PETERS.

[And in like manner, in September Term following, to wit: On the twenty-fourth day of September, 1754, at the said Supream Court, before the said Judges, in pursuance of the aforesaid Act of Parliament, the following Persons:]

Persons' names.	Of what place.	Sacrament, when taken.	
Christopher Shibler,	Philadelphia Co.,	22nd September,	1754
Arnst Kurts.	do.	do.	
John Barned,	do.	11 Septem'r,	1754
Carl Byer,	do.	22 September,	1754
Michael Simon,	do.	do.	
Nicholas Swingle,	Lancaster County,	23 September,	1754
Adam Witrick,	do.	8 September,	1754
Elias Detrick,	Northampton,	1 September,	1754
George Button,	Philadelphia Co.,	22 September,	1754
Andreas Ohl,	do.	25 August,	1754
Daniel Kranenger,	do.	22 September,	1754
Henry Muhlenberg,	do.	15 September,	1754
John Christopher Hartwick,	do.		

And at the the same Court the following persons, being Quakers, or such who conscientiously scruple to take an oath, being also Foreigners, and having complied with the Terms required by the aforesaid act of Parliament, took and subscribed the Qualifications for them appointed by the same act of Parliament, &ca. :

Persons' names.	Of what place.
John Wagle,	Northampton County.
Henry Shank,	Lancaster County.
Henry Lane,	Lancaster County.

Certified by

WILLIAM ALLEN, Esquire, *Chief Justice.*

The foregoing is a true and perfect List from the original Certificate under the Hand of William Allen, Esq'r, remaining in my office.

RICHARD PETERS.

[And in like manner, in April Term following, to wit: On the tenth day of April, 1755, at the said Supream Court, before the said Judges, in pursuance of the aforesaid Act of Parliament, the following Persons, viz:]

Persons' names.	Of what place.	Sacrament, when taken.	
David Giesy,	Northampton Co.,	the 30th March,	1755
Francis Roth,	do.	30 March.	1755
Adam Blank,	do.	do.	
Jacob Timanus,	Philadelphia,	do.	
Valentine Puff,	do.	do.	

Persons' names.	Of what place.	Sacrament' when taken.	
Martin Boger,	Berks,	30 March,	1755
Johannes Forrer,	do	do.	
John Boyer,	do.	29 March,	1755
Philip Fentermaker,	do.	23 March,	1755
Jacob Girardin,	do.	do.	
Samuel Burger,	do.	do.	
Christian Ruth,	Northampton	do.	
Frederick Helwig,	Berks,	do.	
Dewald Carne,	do.	do.	
Joseph Burrey,	do.	do.	
John Hiss,	do.	30 March,	1755
Rudolph Berger,	do.	23 March,	1755
Michael Knab,	do.	30 March,	1755
Christian Doll,	Philadelphia,	6 April,	1755
George Stolnaker,	Northampton,	30 March,	1755
John Ordt,	do.	do.	
Nicholas Swingle,	Berks,	do.	
Peter George,	Bucks,	26 February,	1755
Adam Downey,	do.	30 March,	1755
Christian Kern,	do.	do.	
Godfrey Knous,	Northampton,	31 March,	1755
Frederick Nighat,	do.	3 April,	1755
Nicholas Swingle,	Bucks,	26 January,	1755
George Stout,	Northampton,	30 March,	1755
Adam Lish,	Berks,	do.	
Michael Floras,	Northampton,	8 April,	1755
John Deiter,	Berks,	29 March,	1755
Adam Deshler,	Northampton,	31 March,	1755
H. B. Franks,	York County.	(A Jew.)	
Peter Hittle,	Northampton,	the 8 April,	1755
Adam Heavely,	do.	31 March,	1755
Lawrence Good,	do.	do.	
George Jacob Karn,	do.	3 April,	1755
Henry Wilhelm,	do.	8 April,	1755
Isaac Dalep,	do.	do.	

And at the same Court the following persons, being Quakers, or such who conscientiously scruple to take an oath, being also foreigners, and having complied with the Terms required by the aforesaid act of Parliament, took and subscribed Qualifications for them appointed by the same act of Parliament, &ca.:

Persons' names.	Of what place.
Jost Vollert,	Northampton Co.
Henry Christ,	Berks.
Francis Yost,	do.
Elias Rotter,	do.

Persons' names.	Of what place.
Christian Heller,	Northampton.
Michael Kyper,	do.
Michael Smith,	do.
George Heisler,	Philadelphia.
Christopher Reinwalt,	do.
Martin Brand,	do.
John Etter,	Lancaster.
David Newman,	Philadelphia.
Christ'r Hebener,	do.
George Andrews,	do.
George Kreebel,	do.
David Barringer,	Northampton.
Mathias Bumgardner,	Lancaster.
Valentine Westhoffer	do.
Geo. Headerick,	do.
Christian Vanlashant,	Philadelphia.
William Baker,	City.

Certified by

WILLIAM ALLEN, Esquire, *Chief Justice.*

The foregoing is a true and perfect List, from the original Certificate under the Hand of William Allen, Esquire, remaining in my office.

RICHARD PETERS.

———

[And in like manner, in September Term following, to wit: On the twenty-fourth day of September, 1755, at the said Supream Court, before the said Judges, in pursuance of the aforesaid Act of Parliament, the following persons, viz:]

Persons' names.	Of what place.	Sacrament, when taken.	
Henry Lorats,	Philadelphia C'y, the	21 September,	1755
Reinhot Abendshen,	Berks,	31 August,	1755
Graft Hiner,	do.	21 September,	1775
Frederick Cressman,	Philadelphia,	24 September,	1755
Abraham Ornt,	do.	21 September,	1755
John Graff,	City,	14 September,	1755
Albright Straus,	Berks,	24 September,	1755
Jacob Chryster,	City,	14 September,	1755
Christopher Diekenshat,	Philadelphia,	31. August,	1755
George Swinehart,	Berks,	14 September,	1755
Henry Newkirk,		do.	
Michael Swinehart,	Philadelphia,	do.	
Ludwick Pickle,	do.	do.	
Christ'r Newman,	do.	22 Sept.,	1755
Nicholas Yost,	Berks,	21 Sept'r,	1755

Persons' names.	Of what place.	Sacrament, when taken	
Andrew Smith,	Philadelphia,	22 Sept.,	1755
John Spyker,	Lancaster,	16 Septem.,	1755
George Swank,	Philadelphia,	23 September,	1755
Mathias Keler.	do.	22 Septem'r,	1755
Valentine Gerber,	Lancaster,	21 Septem'r,	1755
Conradt Beam,	Berks,	3 Septem'r,	1755
Nicholas Swenk,	Philadelphia,	24 Septem'r.	1755
Conradt Speech,	do.	23 Septem'r,	1755
John Gates,	do.	31 August,	1755
Philip Yost,	do.	22 Septem'r,	1755
John Shneeke,	Lancaster,	31 Aug.,	1755
Nicholas Martin,	do.	21 Sept.,	1755
Casper Gore,	do.	5 August,	1755
Philip Gephart,	Berks,	27 July,	1755
Henry Shewen,	do.	do	
Sebastian Stain,	Lancaster,	do.	

And at the same Court, the following Persons being Quakers, or such who Conscientiously scruple to take an Oath, being also Foreigners, and having complied with the Terms required by the aforesaid Act of Parliament, took and subscribed the Qualifications for them appointed by the same Act of Parliamen, &ca. :

Persons' names.	Of what place.
Philip Linhear,	Lancaster County.
Andrew Boyer,	Philadelphia.
John Buckaus,	do.
Samuel Filbert,	Berks.
Stephen Bernard,	do.
Peter Hyster,	Philadelphia,
Tobias Bekle,	Lancaster.
Yost Olewine,	Bucks.
Jacob Keene,	Berks.
Fred. Geerhart,	do.
Peter Oufensanberger,	Lancaster.
David Breack,	do.
John Gotleck,	do.
Lazarus Winger,	Berks.
John Meyer,	do.
Jacob Miller,	do.
George Stump,	Philadelphia.
Jacob Greater,	Berks County.
Henry Star,	Berks County.
Peter Knop,	do.
Jacob Whistler,	Lancaster.

Persons' names.	Of what place.
Daniel Reehldown,	Lancaster.
Gerhart Etter,	do.
John Hargarater,	Berks.
Valentine Gross,	Lancaster.
Daniel Burneman,	Philadelphia.
Christopher Fry,	Lancaster.
Peter Becksaker,	do.
Christian Palmer,	do.
Henry Smith,	do.
Frederick Keysele,	dc.
Valentine Miller,	do.
Christ'an Richeop,	Philadelphia.
George Lesh,	Lancaster.

Certified by

WILLIAM ALLEN, Esquire, *Chief Justice.*

The foregoing is a true and perfect List, taken from the original Certificate, under the Hand of William Allen, Esquire, remaining in my office.

RICHARD PETERS.

———

[And in like manner, in April Term following, to wit: On the 10 day of April, 1756, at the said Supream Court, before the said Judges, in pursuance of the aforesaid act of Parliament, the following persons:]

Persons' names.	Of what township.	And of what county.
Rudolph Honakei,	Rockhill Township,	Bucks County.
Jacob Miner,	Easton,	Easton.
Martin Weybreythe,	Manhiem,	Lancaster.
Henry Schweitzer,	Manhiem,	Lancaster.

Certified by

WILLIAM ALLEN, Esquire, *Chief Justice.*

The foregoing is a true and perfect list, taken from the original Certificate under the hand of William Allen, Esquire, remaining in my office.

RICHARD PETERS.

———

[And in like manner, September term following, to wit: On the 24th September, 1756, at the said Supream Court, before the s'd Judges, in pursuance of the aforesaid act of Parliament, the following persons:]

Jurors' names.	Jurors' names.
Philip Brown,	John Philip Heist.
George Lintz,	

And at the same Court, the following persons being Quakers, or such who conscientiously scruple to take an Oath, being also Foreigners, and having complied with the Terms required by the aforesaid Act of Parliament, took and subscribed the Qualifications for them appointed by the same act of Parliament, &ca. :

Affirmers' names.	Affirmers' names.
Henry Meyer,	. John Williams.
George Telp,	

Certified by

WILLIAM ALLEN, Esquire, *Chief Justice.*

The foregoing is a true and perfect List, taken from the original Certificate, under the Hand of William Allen, Esq'r, remaining in my office.

RICHARD PETERS.

———

[And in like manner, in April Term following, to wit: On the 10th day of April, 1757, at the said Supream Court, before the said Judges, in pursuance of the aforesaid Act of the Parliament, the following persons, viz:]

Jurors' names.	Jurors' names.
Jacob Ehrenzeller,	Adam Falker,
Jacob Heauke,	Jacob Dondle,
John Nicholas Heist,	George Amstmeyer,
John Seidle,	Conrad Bapp,
George Kentz,	John Conrad Schweighauser,
Andrew Nappinger,	David Shaffer,
Goliffe Seigle,	Christop'r HansMann.

And at the same Court, the following persons being Quakers or such who conscientiously scruple to take an oath, being also Foreigners, and having complied with the Terms required * * * by the aforesaid Act of Parliament, took and subscribed the Qualifications for them appointed by the same Act of Parliament, &ca. :

Affirmers' names.	Affirmers' names.
Peter Everly,	Ulrick Staley,
Adolph Meyer,	Teterick Marshall.
Jacob Everly,	

Certified by

WILLIAM ALLEN, Esquire,
Chief Justice, &ca.

The foregoing is a true and perfect List from the original Certificate under the Hand of William Allen, Esquire, remaining in my office.

RICHARD PETERS.

[And in like manner, in September Term following, to wit: On the twenty-fourth day of September, 1757, at the said Supream Court, before the said Judges, in pursuance of the aforesaid Act of Parliament, the following Persons:]

Jurors' names.	Jurors' names.
Michael Thies,	Rudolph Oberling.
Michael Hoffman,	Peter Knight.
Martin Letterman,	Antony Lerets.

And at the same Court, the following Persons being Quakers, or such who Conscientiously scruple to take an Oath, being also Foreigners, and having complied with the terms required by the aforesaid Act of Parliament, Took and subscribed the Qualifications for them appointed by the same Act of Parliament, &ca., viz:

Affirmers' names.	Affirmers' names.
John Cook.	John Weaver,
John Dedier,	Caper Dumerneilt,
Henry Leshier,	David Dumerneilt,
Lewis Caslar.	

Certified by

WILLIAM ALLEN, Esquire, *Chief Justice*, *&ca.*

The foregoing is a true and perfect List, taken from the original Certificate under the Hand of William Allen, Esquire, remaining in my office.

RICHARD PETERS.

———

[And in like manner, in April Term following, to wit: On the tenth day of April, 1758, at the said Supream Court, before the said Judges, in pursuance of the aforesaid Act of Parliament, the following Persons:]

Jurors' names.	Jurors' names.
Anthony Forrest.	Baltzer Erlach,
Adam Spaan,	Catharine Koch,
Gabriel Riecher.	John Unfersaht,
Alexander Sheffer,	John Frederick Rohr,
William Bauman,	Joseph Hister,
George Spreeker.	Jacob Isaac,
Martin Tomy,	Valentine Shallos.

N. B.—There were no Affirmers at this Court.

Certified by

WILLIAM ALLEN, Esquire, *Chief Justice*, *&ca.*

The foregoing is a true and perfect List taken from the original certificate, under the Hand of John Kinsey, Esq'r, remaining in my office.

RICHARD PETERS.

[And in like manner, in September Term following, to wit: On the twenty-fifth day of September, 1758, at the said Supream Court, before the said Judges, in Pursuance of the aforesaid Act of Parliament the following Persons, viz:]

Jurors' names.

Abraham Brosis,
Nicholas Sysinger,
Henry Haun,
Martin Kaust,
Andones Engel,
Isaac Young,
Peter Rupp,
Henry Rietmeyer,
George Shultz,
Henry Deacanhalt,
Michael Partius,

Jurors' names.

Christian Orendolf,
Adam Sleeger,
Everhart Martin,
Antony Derder,
Michael Kauble,
Conrad Bem,
Jno. Adam Miller,
John Geo. Rees,
George Kast,
Geo. Frederick Beyer.

No affirmers this Term.

Certified by

WILLIAM ALLEN, Esq'r, *Chief Justice, &ca.*

The foregoing is a true and perfect List from the original Certificate under the Hand of William Allen, Esq'r, remaining in my office.

RICHARD PETERS.

[And in like manner in April Term, following to wit: On the tenth day of April, 1759, at the said Supream Court, before the said Judges, in pursuance of the aforesaid Act of Parliament, the following Persons:]

Jurors' names.

Paul Bailliet,
Michael Spiegle,
Michael Newhart,
Michael Karcher,
Negro Fry,

Jurors' names.

Andrew Brechel,
Christian Homer,
Catharine Kaufman,
John Egle.

And at the same Court the following persons, being Quakers, or such who conscientiously scruple to take an oath, being also foreigners & having complied with the Terms required by the aforesaid act of Parliament, took and subscribed the Qualifications for them appointed by the same act of Parliament, &ca:

Affirmers' names.

Stophel Hanley,
Stophel Haimsell,
Gregorius Maister,
Christian Fernstermaker,
Bastian Benner,
George Schlosser,

Affirmers' names.

Peter Keechline,
Baltzer Yaigle,
John Bectell,
Ulrick Hansberger,
Martin Karchar,
Benedict Kayman.

Certified by

WILLIAM ALLEN, Esqr., *Chief Justice, &ca.*

The foregoing is a true and perfect List from the original Certificate under the Hand of William Allen, Esquire, remaining in my office.

RICHARD PETERS.

[And in like manner, in September term following, to wit: On the twenty-fourth of September, 1759, at the said Supream Court, before the said Judges, in pursuance of the aforesaid act of Parliament, the following Persons:]

Jurors' names.

George Loutz,
Nicholas Boyer,
Jacob Sharen,
Peter Feather,
Jacob Yaiger,
Peter Haas,
George Geisler,
Lodowick Tillinger,
Martin Heekendorn,
John Bishop,
John Moll,
Jacob Begtol,
Henry Hoerer,

Jurors' names.

Durst Fisler,
Adam Kookert,
Nicholas Francis,
Michael Fleese,
John George Myerly,
David Myerly,
Henry Radeback,
John Nicholas Ensminger,
John Nicholas Hermicke,
John Alright Hackenmiller,
John Sneider,
Jacob Hookart,
Christian Laugbaugh.

And at the same Court the following persons, being Quakers, or such who conscientiously scruple to take an Oath, being also Foreigners, and having complied with the terms required by the aforesaid Act of Parliament, took and subscribed the Qualifications for them appointed by the same Act of Parliament, &ca.

Affirmers' names.

Hieronimus Henning,
Michael Lodwick,
John Pott,
Lodowick Imbler,
Casper Mantz,
Philip Greenwalt,
George Yoke,
Abraham Immoberstake,
Bastian Levan,
      Certified by

Affirmers' names.

Peter Shitz,
Frederick Maynard,
Conrad Weaver,
Adam Goos,
John Titmore,
Michael Diffiderfer,
John Taylor,
Christian Shibely.

WILLIAM ALLEN, esquire,
Chief Justice, &ca.

The foregoing is a true and perfect List from the original Certificate under the Hand of William Allen, Esquire, remaining in my office.

RICHARD PETERS.

[And in like manner, in April Term following, to wit: On the tenth day of April, 1760, at the said Supream Court, before the said Judges, in pursuance of the aforesaid Act of Parliament, the following Persons, viz:]

Jurors' names.

Rudolph Breneison,
Michael Reuter,
Gerrhart Hibsham,
Johannes Ernst,
John Philip Burkhard,
John George Stone,
Frederick Wirth,
Henry Steel,
Lorenze Marquetand,
William Bush,
John Nicholas Job,
Leonard May,
John George Sneider,
Michael Ohl,
John Casper Graffe,
Henry Giekert,
Adam Boone,
Frederick From,
Mathias Weaver,
Henry Sauer,
Jacob Barge,
Christopher Graffe,
Peter Dick,
Henry Brunner,
Peter Deal,
Peter Paris,
Abraham Wild,
Emanuel Fred'k Wreckerle,
Jacob Kohler,
Martin Icleberger,
Peter Rapp,
Michael Kuhns,
John Wolf,
John Jacob Shoemaker,
Henrick Wolf,
Winebert Tshoudee,
Jacob Wilhelm,
Ann Catharina Wilhelm,
Frederick Nungesser,
Jacob Gratz,
Mathias Kern,

Jurors' names.

Michael Schlonecker,
Michael Schlonecker, Jun'r,
Gebhart Berthold,
John William Hoffman,
Conrad Brown,
Diel Bauer,
Martin Kind,
Joseph Welshance,
Martin Danner,
George Michael Kam,
John Gittinger,
John Shultz,
Nicholas Kintzer,
Jacob Dunder,
George Wolf,
Jacob Bricker,
John Hoy,
Adam Sticker,
Peter Koker,
Henry Proctor,
Adam Hambright,
Conrad Hyssley,
Leonard Leighner,
Leonard Abel,
Christian Milheim,
George Christian Sinn,
Michael Karl,
Frederick Gilwicks,
Nicholas Bedinger,
Maria Catharine Albright,
George Mayer,
Conrad Amma,
Jacob Zeigler,
Nicholas Wolfhart,
John Beisser,
Jacob Deitrick,
Nicholas Herner,
Lawrence Rees,
Philip Dick,
Adam Probst,
John Sawler.

Jurors' names.

Petriem Weiland,
Michael Klein,
Christopher Henry Reinhold,
John Michael Amweg,
Martin Burkholder,
Martin Dresback,
Leonard Mayer,
Frederick Mayer,
Mathias Kelchner,
Deter Uler,
Philip Zeigler,
Philip Entler,
George Deer,
Lucas Rous,
William Koch,
George Burkhard,
William Shimel,
John Beeber,
Michael Kernise,
Peter Haus,
Nicholas Mayer,
Harman Mohr,
David Duckener,
Henry Young,

Jurors' names.

Godfried Bockius,
Lodowick Sarmer,
George Bush,
Andreas Sheffer,
Christian Grubber,
Philip Meeth,
John George Eppely,
Paul Reiser,
Martin Fisher,
Christian Reinhart Uhl,
Ulrick Zollinger,
Jacob Maag,
Jacob Kagy,
John Henry Katz,
William Hains,
Melchior Smith,
Michael Radeback,
Martin Becker,
Henry Kik,
Peter Buger,
Christian Cassel,
Henry William Steigle,
George Becker,
Henry Souter.

And at the same Court the following Persons being Quakers, or such who conscientiously scruple to take an oath, being also Foreigners, and Laving complied with the terms required by the aforesaid act of Parliament, took and subscribed the Qualifications for them appointed by the same act of Parliament, &ca:

Affirmers' names.

Rudolph Naglee,
John Geer,
Adam Cutwalt,
George Hartman,
Frederick Shous,
Conrad Streiber,
George Frederick,
Jacob Peck,
John Nicholl,
Jacob Rich,
George Weller.

Affirmers' names.

George Sholtz,
Christian Sleighty,
William Rutt,
Frederick Post,
Leonard Bidleman,
John Bitting,
Elias Hummell,
Jacob Grove,
Francis Michael Bishop,
Jacob Stove.

Certified by

WILLIAM ALLEN, Esquire,
Chief Justice, &ca.

The foregoing is a true and perfect List, taken from the original Certificate under the Hand of William Allen, Esqr., remaining in my office.

[And in like manner, in September Term following, to wit: On the twenty-fourth day of September, 1760, at the said Supream Court, before the said Judges in pursuance of the aforesaid Act of Parliament, the, following Persons, viz:]

Jurors' names.	County.	Sacrament, when taken.
Jacob Ekert,	Berks County,	18th September, 1760
Jacob Focks,	Philadelphia,	7 September, 1760
Martin Alstat,	Berks,	do.
Nicholas Alstat,	do.	do.
Michael Feithorn,	do.	14 September, 1760
Adam Epler,	do.	10 August, 1760
John Cunnus,	Berks,	7 September, 1760
Philip Faass,	Philad'a,	21 September, 1760
Peter Buker,	Lancaster,	do.
Philip Runk,	do.	do.
Casper Yost,	do.	do.
John Browbraker,	do.	do.
Henry Woolfkull,	do.	do.
William Giger,	Philadelphia,	7 September, 1760
Christopher Wagman,	Lancaster,	17 August, 1760
Abraham Sherper,	Berks,	10 August, 1760
Conrad Mark,	Lancaster,	14 September, 1760
Christian Hollinger,	do.	do.
Melchior Haffaa,	Berks,	do.
Philip Erpff,	Lancaster,	21 September, 1760
Christo'r Weidman,	do.	6 July, 1760
Lawrence Householder,	do.	do.
Michael Kraus,	Berks,	14 September, 1760
Peter Fisher,	do.	7 September, 1760
Paul Durst,	do.	do.
Conrad Keller	do.	do.
Jno. Fred. Handshuh,	Philadelphia,	21 September, 1760
Frederick Yaisser,	Lancaster,	31 August, 1760
Michael Kelkner,	Berks,	14 September, 1760
Michael Zeister,	Berks,	21 September, 1760
Frederick Spiegle,	Northampton,	6 September, 1760
George Nutz,	Berks,	14 September, 1760
George Schuhntz,	do.	21 September, 1760
Jacob Schuhntz.	do.	do.
William Figel,	Northampton,	6 September, 1760
Matthias Burgher,	Lancaster,	31 August, 1760

Jurors' names.	County.	Sacrament, when taken.	
Jacob Boyer,	Berks,	7 September,	1760
Matthias Deter,	do.	do.	
George Hoyle,	Lancaster,	6 July,	1760
Frederick Walkick,	Berks,	14 September,	1760
John George Meyer,	Philadelphia,	7 September,	1760
John Liser,	Lancaster,	31 August,	1760
Daniel Rudy,	do.	do.	
Martin Shriner,	do.	do.	
Martin Verntheusel,	do.	do.	
John Nicholas Kurtz,	Philadelphia,	21 September,	1760
Conrad Bonner,	do.	7 September,	1760
George Sonn,	York,	1 July,	1760
John Shmeck,	Berks,	20 July,	1760
John George Fitler,	Philadelphia,	7 September,	1760
Nicholas Shubert,	Northampton,	21 September,	1760
Jacob Becker,	Philadelphia,	do.	
Charles Hefflin,	Berks,	14 September,	1760
George Volck,	do.	do.	
Martin Offner,	Lancaster,	24 August,	1760
Philip Moser,	Philadelphia,	21 September,	1760
Fælix Hurlieman,	do.	do.	
Henry Arnt,	do.	do.	
Thomas Schley,	Frederick, in Maryland,	22 July,	1760
George Hacker,	Lancaster,	6 July,	1760
George Whitman,	do.	do.	
George Rieger,	Berks,	14 September,	1760
Wendal Becker,	Philadelphia,	21 September,	1760
Barnaby Becker,	do.	do.	
Jno. Nicholas Handwerk,	Northampton,	31 Aug't,	1760
Conrad Been,	Berks,	14 Sept.,	1760
Conrad Gilbert,	Philad'a,	23 Sept.,	1760
Bernard Gilbert,	do.	do.	
Ludwick Herring,	do.	do.	
Christopher Hienkle,	do.	do.	
Daniel Nyer,	do.	do.	
Jacob Carver,	Philad'a,	7 Sept.,	1760
Andreas Kickeline,	Bucks,	20 Sept.,	1760
Jacob Rees,	do.	7 Sept.,	1760
John Walker,	Philadelphia,	21 Sept.,	1760

And at the same Court the following Persons being Quakers or such who conscientiously scruple to take an oath, being also Foreigners, and having complied with the Terms required b the aforesaid act of Parliament, took and subscribed the Qualifications aforesaid for them appointed by the same act of Parliament, &ca. :

Persons' names.	Of what place.
Frederick Lienback,	Berks.
John Lienback,	do.
Henry Lienback,	do.
John Killis,	Philad'a.
Michael Hofman,	do.
John Keller,	Northampton.
Stephen Dysher,	Berks.
Jacob Tribblebess,	do.
Conrad Manismit,	do.
Jacob Whitmore,	Lancaster.
Jacob Hoyle,	do.
Christian Good,	do.
Leonard Cline,	do.
Detrick Coquelin,	do.
Jno. Coquelin,	do.
Valentine Bowman,	do.
Fred. Waidle,	do.
Sebastian Keller,	do.
John Tendler,	do.
John Stokey,	do.
Peter Little,	York.
Geo. Schwantz,	Lancaster.
Henry Yunken,	Philadelphia.
Certified by	WILLIAM ALLEN, Esq'r,
	Chief Justice, &ca.

The foregoing is a true and perfect List, taken from the original certificate under the Hand of William Allen, Esqr., remaining in my office.

RICHARD PETERS.

[At a Supream Court held at Philadelphia, before William Allen and William Coleman, Esquires, Judges of the said Court, the tenth and eleventh days of April, in the Year of our Lord one thousand seven hundred and sixty-one, between the Hours of Nine and twelve of the Clock of the forenoon of the same day, the following subscribing persons being foreigners :]

Persons' names.	Of what place.	Sacrament, when taken.	
Matthias Lopald,	Philad'a County,	22d March,	1761
John Frederick Hagner,	do.	do.	
William Strainer,	do.	do.	
John George Laib,	do.	do.	
John Jacob Rode,	do.	do.	
John Weisman,	do.	do.	

Persons' names.	Of what place.	Sacrament, when taken.	
Matthias Smith,	Berks,	22d March,	1761
Peter Gottshall,	Lancaster,	4 April,	1761
Geo. Frederick Baish,	do.	do.	
John Appleman,	York,	22 March,	1761
Conrad Werns,	Lancaster,	do.	
Jacob Graff, Jun'r,	Philadelphia,	22d March,	1761
Sebastian Muffler,	do.	do.	
Andreas Holsbaun,	Lancaster,	do.	
George Weber,	do.	do.	
David Schurck,	do.	do.	
Philip Rhode,	do.	do.	
George Werns,	do.	do.	
Gerhard Kafroth,	do.	24 March,	1761
Jacob Dummin,	do.	do.	
Henry Fedder,	do.	do.	
George Yund,	do.	23 March,	1761
Johannes Schneider,	Berks,	22 do.	
David Law, Orange Co.,	North Carolina,	do.	
Johannes Hoffman,	Berks,	do.	
Ulrich Radmaker,	do.	do.	
John Andrew Miser-smith,	Philadelphia,	22 March,	1761
Henry Kepple,	do.	do.	
John Andrew Rohr,	do.	22 February,	1761
Herman Weber,	Berks,	1 April,	1761
Jacob Stein,	do.	1 April,	1761
Conrad Schneider,	Berks,	1 April,	1761
Herman Reik,	do.	22 March,	1761
George Waggoner,	do.	1 April,	do.
Wilhelm Leymeister,	do.	22 March,	1761
Christian Hoffman,	do.	do.	
John Althouse,	do.	1 April,	1761
Peter Ruth,	Berks,	15 March,	do.
Jacob Bordner,	do.	7 April,	1761
Valentine Mayer,	do.	do.	
George Wolf,	do.	do.	
George Canter,	do.	do.	
Christian Book,	Lancaster,	22 March,	1761
Abraham Riblet,	do.	do.	
John Bentz,	do.	do.	
William Hedrick,	Berks,	do.	
Yost Hedrick,	do.	do.	
Martin Ernhold,	do.	do.	
Bernard Sheretele,	do.	do.	
Yost Shoemaker,	do.	do.	

Persons' names.	Of what place.	Sacrament, when taken.	
Valentine Mogle,	Berks,	29 March,	1761
Ludwick Saman,	do.	do.	
Eberhard Geshwind,	do.	do.	
Ulrick Bagentoss,	do.	1 April,	do.
Henry Graber,	do.	22 March,	do.
Michael Shower,	do.	do.	
Herman Hassinger,	do.	5 April,	do.
Jacob Wagner,	do.	do.	
Christopher Wagner,	do.	do.	
Jacob Lanciscus,	do.	do.	
Rudolph Gurhart,	do.	do.	
Jacob Young,	do.	do.	
Victor Speiss,	do.	do.	
Philip Reezer,	do.	do.	
Philip Lowbenback,	do.	do.	
George Yoh,	do.	do.	
Christian Weeks,	do.	do.	
Conrad Keller,	do.	do.	
Adam Gerhart,	do.	do.	
Jacob Wyler,	do.	do.	
Yost Wagner,	Berks,	5 April,	1761
John Shock,	do.	29 March,	1761
Nicholas Fringer,	Lancaster,	3 April,	do.
Jacob Stuke,	Philadelphia,	22 March,	do.
John Engle Brown.	Berks,	do.	
Christopher Schaub,	Lancaster,	1 April,	1761
Peter Frankhouser,	do.	do.	
John Ryswick,	Northampton,	22 March,	1761
Christopher Keiser,	Berks,	do.	
John Wurman,	Bucks,	8 March,	1761
Frederick Jackis,	Berks,	22 March,	1761
Reinhard Roreback,	do.	do.	
Nicholas Marritt,	Lancaster,	19 March,	1761
Martin Spickler,	do.	do.	
Henry Dehoff,	do.	29 March,	1761
Ludwick Beker,	Lancaster,	19 March,	1761
Peter Gubelius,	do.	29 March,	1761
Jacob Ran,	Berks,	6 April,	1761
Leonard Hockgenug,	do.	7 do.	
Bernard Feather,	Lancaster,	22 March,	1761
George Reiner,	Northampton,	29 March,	1761
Anthony Lambright,	Berks,	1 April,	1761
Matthias Stout.	Berks.	22 March,	1761
Valentine Schneider,	Lancaster,	do.	
Philip Stober,	do.	do.	

Persons' names.	Of what place.	Sacrament, when taken.	
Casper Mesner,	Lancaster,	22 March,	1761
Christian Mesner,	do.	do.	
George Weaver,	do.	29 do.	
Matthew Meyer,	Philadelphia,	22 do.	
Paul Kober,	do.	22 February,	1761
Christian Ruth,	Berks,	1 April,	do.
Nicholas. Klee,	do.	22 March,	176:
George Mettler,	do.	7 April,	do.
Sebastian Crime,	do.	29 March,	do.
Jacob Crime,	do.	do.	
John Yost,	Philadelphia,	28 do.	
Jacob Gickert,	Berks,	3 April,	do.
Peter Fitzer,	do	22 March,	176:
Samuel Kuth,	do.	6 April,	176:
George Beck,	York,	22 March,	176:
Jacob Schneider,	do.	do.	
Jacob Bott,	do.	5 April,	176:
Michael Ruth,	Berks,	15 March,	176:
John Bullman,	do.	do.	
Philip Adam Sherman,	do.	do.	
Jacob Ruth,	do.	do.	
John Hehart,	do.	do.	
Michael Miller,	do.	do.	
Michael Traxell,	Northampton,	22 do.	
Jno. Christ'r Spengler,	Berks.	7 April,	176
John Mettauer,	Lancaster,	22 March,	176
Henry Reech,	do.	do.	
Henry Hanse,	do.	19 do.	
Matthias Hoffer,	do.	15 February,	176
Michael Wolf,	do.	19 March,	176
Adam Keener,	do.	15 February,	176
William Spotz,	do.	7 April,	176
Jno. Bernard Frank,	do.	29 March,	176
Conrad Farsnaught,	do.	22 do.	
Martin Schwenk,	Northampton,	23 March,	176
Jacob Smith,	do.	do.	
George Pfotezer,	Lancaster,	8 February,	176
Samuel Wolf,	do.	do.	
Daniel Huber,	do.	do.	
Jacob Miller,	do.	do.	
Christopher Reem,	do.	22 March,	176
Philip Seng,	do.	do.	
Philip Dennius,	do.	7 April,	176
John Bonnett,	do.	do.	
Peter Wolff,	do.	do.	

Persons' names.	Of what place.	Sacrament, when taken.	
Nicholas Schriener,	Philadelphia,	9 April,	1761
Nicholas Gampert,	do.	do.	
John Mohn,	Berks,	15 March,	1761
William Ermel,	do.	22 do.	
Nicholas Schappert,	do .	do.	
William Marks,	do.	do.	
George Weidner,	do.	7 April,	1761
Baltzer Myerly,	do.	22 March.	1761
Henry Geiger,	Northampton,	23 March,	1761
Martin Ginginger,	do.	22 do.	
Philip Henry Rapp,	Philadelphia,	do.	
Peter Herr,	Northampton,	do.	
Andrew Hertz,	do.	do.	
Melchor Debler,	Berks,	do.	
George Haffner,	do.	8 April,	1761
Abraham Keefer,	do.	6 March,	1761
Henry Sowass,	do.	do.	
George Sheffer	do.	do.	
Michael Cline	Bucks,	22 do.	
Casper Nype,	do.	6 do.	
Martin Crafft,	Berks,	22 do.	
John Beber,	do.	5 April,	1761
Dewald Beber,	do.	do.	
Ulrick Hartman,	Philadelphia,	23 March	1761
Rudolph Kidwiller,	Bucks	5 April	1761
Charles Witz,	Philadelphia,	22 March	do.
Jacob Liebegut,	do.	do.	
Michael Brand,	do.	do.	
Melchior Sheener,	Philadelphia,	1 April,	do.
Ludwick Shick,	do.	do.	
Peter Howg,	Philadelphia,	28th March,	1761
Martin Yorger,	do.	1 April	do.
Philip Adam Dieler,	Lancaster,	29 March	do.
John Smidt,	Philadelphia	23	do.
Christian Sitzman,	Bucks,	do.	
Abraham Hauser	Philadelphia,	23 do.	
John Greenwalt,	do.	22 do.	
Peter Burkholder,	Northampton,	do.	
Jacob Rumman,	Philadelphia,	23 do.	
David Deshler,	Northampton,	15 do.	
George Henry Joseph,	Bucks,	22 do.	
Casper Slatter,	do.	23 do.	
George Shoul,	Philadelphia,	23 March,	1761
Jacob Kopp,	do.	15 do.	
Jacob Schyck,	do.	do.	

Persons' names.	Of what place.	Sacrament, when taken	
Michael Horlacher,	Bucks,	9 April,	1761
Bless Weiber,	Philadelphia,	22 March,	1761
Philip Behm,	Philadelphia,	15 April,	1761
Wigand Pannibecker,	do.	15 March,	1761
John Nicholas Young,	do.	22 March,	1761
Ludwick Zeigler,	Lancaster,	do.	
Melchior Barr,	Northampton,	23 do.	
Ulrick Spinner	Bucks,	22 do.	
Henry Swartz,	Berks,	do.	
Mich'l Hartman Dillo,	Northampton,	do.	
Christ'r Goodman,	do.	25 March,	1761
Geo. Shamback,	Philadelphia,	28 March,	1761
Daniel Rot,	Northampton,	15 March,	1761
Daniel Traxell,	do	do.	
Christ'r Berkenbeil,	Philadelphia,	22 March,	1761
Philip Spear,	do.	23	
Henry Wolf,	Berks,	22	
Andreas Boyer,	Northampton,	do.	
George Kershner,	do.	6 April,	176.
George Rinehard,	do.	do.	
Abraham Dannehower,	do.	do.	
Frederick Sheffer,	do.	8 April,	176
Henry Huber,	Bucks,	22 March,	176
John Waspie,	Philadelphia,	do.	
John Jacob Miller,	do.	22 do.	
Francis Westgo,	Northampton,	23 do.	
Nicholas Rotenberger,	do.	do.	
Adam Berger,	Lancaster,	22 March,	176
Christopher Barr,	Northampton,	do.	
Henry Brunner,	do.	6 April,	do
Jacob Engle,	Philadelphia,	22 March,	176
Andrew Honetta,	do.	1 April,	do
Henry Fetter,	Northampton,	22 March,	do
Andrew Erdman,	do.	6 April,	do
Michael Sieder,	do.	do.	
Baltzer, Boyle,	do.	do.	
Henry Ekell,	Bucks,	8	dc
George Schellmeir,	Philadelphia,	15 March,	176
Michael Putts,	Bucks,	5 April	176
Christian Shukes,	do.	do.	
Nicholas Wierpack,	do.	do.	
Jacob Overpeck,	Berks,	5 April,	176
Christian Düy,	Philadelphia,	22 March,	176
Matthias Foltz,	do.	do.	
Christian Schneider,	do.	do.	

Persons' names.	Of what place.	Sacrament, when taken.	
Henry Rees,	Northampton,	23 March,	1761
Jacob Sieder,	Berks,	22 do.	
John Groce,	do.	do.	
Valentine Stienmetz,	Northampton,	6 April,	1761
Christian Donnacre,	Philadelphia,	22 February,	1761
Jno. Remigius Spiegle,	do.	22 March,	1761
Leonard Frely,	Philadelphia,	do.	
John Peter Wittberger,	do.	10 April,	do.
George Adam Gaab,	do.	22 March,	do.
George Keemer.	do.	do.	
John Haberacker,	Berks,	7 April,	1761
Nicholas Shitfer,	do.	15 March,	do.
Jno. Nicholas Traxell,	Northampton,	22 March,	do.
Jno. Sneider,	do.	do.	
Ulrick Flickinger,	do.	do.	
Philip Upp,	Lancaster,	29	do.
Durst Thoma,	do.	7 April,	1761
George Stoler,	do.	do.	
Frederick Wolfesberger,	do.	do.	
Jno. Meyer,	do.	do.	
Martin Hitfelfinger,	do.	do.	
Jacob Dui,	do.	do.	
Adam Bollman,	do.	do.	
Yost Hoffman,	do.	do.	
Peter Lamb,	Berks,	15 March,	1761
Adam Hickman,	do.	22	do.
Jno. Adam Shneider,	Philadelphia,	6 April,	1761
Yost Sterback,	York,	5 do.	
Jacob Yost,	Philadelphia,	22 March,	1761
Samuel Seger,	Northampton,	5 April,	1761
Christian Seger,	do.	do.	
Christian Berger,	Berks,	1 do.	
Lawrence Kehnly,	Northampton,	5 do.	
Nicholas Long,	Berks,	7 do.	
John Raeber,	do.	1 do.	
Jacob Hubler,	Berks,	7 April.	
John Schop,	do.	do.	
Adam Huey,	Northampton,	5 do.	
Tobias Retter,	Lancaster,	29 March,	1761
George Shwingle,	Lancaster,	5 April,	1761
Abraham Netf,	do.	do.	
Jacob Netf,	do.	do.	
Henry Moke,	Lancaster,	30 March,	1761
Andreas Mohr,	do.	29 do.	
Casper Ipa,	do.	do.	

Persons' names.	Of what place.	Sacrament, when take	
John Matthias Albert,	Lancaster,	29 March,	17(
Nicholas Hess,	Philadelphia,	22 do.	
Jacob Eyler,	do.	do.	
Christop'r Steigh,	Lancaster,	22nd March,	17(
Henry Shenk,	do.	do.	
Killian Moy,	Berks,	do.	
John Endres,	Lancaster,	3 April,	17(
Michael Hentzell,	Berks,	22 March,	do.
Conrad Ernst,	do.	do.	
Mich'l Oberly,	Lancaster,	23 do.	
Nicholas Lesher,	do.	1 April,	17(
Jacob Kuhl,	Berks,	22 March,	d(
Nicholas Holder, Sen'r,	do.	do.	
Nicholas Holder, Jun.,	do.	do.	
John Henry Cline,	Philadelphia,	do.	
Jacob Genslin,	do.	do.	
Martin Noll,	do.	do.	
Jno. Waldschmith,	Lancaster,	do.	
Jacob Diek,	Berks,	7 April.	17(
George Diehl,	do.	do.	
David Rien,	do.	do.	
Adam Wagner,	do.	do.	
Jacob Bucher,	do.	do.	
William Miller,	do.	do.	
Wolfgang Hackner,	do.	do.	
Frederick Goodhart,	do.	do.	
Julius Kerper,	do.	do.	
Jacob Librook,	do.	do.	
Christ'r Gotshall,	do.	do.	
Gabriel Schopp,	Berks,	7 April,	176
Christ'r Smith,	do.	do.	
George Rehm,	do.	do.	
Michael Fetter,	do.	do.	
Valentine Himalbarger,	do.	22 March,	176
Catharina Schuen,	do.	6 April,	"
Yost Tobie,	do.	29 March,	"
Jacob Hoffman,	do.	do.	
Martin Kersener,	do.	1 April,	176
Adam Stumra.	do.	do.	
Caspar Lerk,	do.	do.	
Michael Giessleman,	York,	1 April,	176
Daniel Dehl,	do.	do.	
John Glaidy,	do.	5 April,	176
Sebastian Stohler,	Lancaster,	29 March,	176
John Feltman,	do.	22 do.	

Persons' names.	Of what place.	Sacrament, when taken.	
Daniel Dewald,	York,	22 March,	1761
Jacob Wagner,	do.	do.	
John Jacob Ottinger,	do.	do.	
Jno. Herick Cline,	do.	do.	
Francis Noll,	do.	do.	
George Ness,	do.	do.	
Jacob Rudisilly,	do.	do.	
Michael Wommer,	Berks,	5 April,	1761
John Wolf,	York,	do.	
George Gerrnant,	Berks,	22 March,	1761
John Zinn,	York,	do.	
Jacob Meyer,	do.	do.	
Peter Obb,	York,	22nd March,	1761
Peter Streher,	do.	5 April,	1761
Jacob Epler,	Berks,	3 do.	
Peter Harbine,	do.	do.	
Philip Mahomer,	do.	do.	
Christian Albright,	do.	do.	
John Faust,	do.	do.	
George Ressler,	do.	do.	
Daniel Zachariss,	do.	do.	
John Mich'l Womer,	do.	do.	
Valentine Epler,	do.	do.	
Jacob Albright,	Berks,	3 April.	
Christian Oldhouse,	do.	do.	
George Gafft,	York,	22 March,	1761
Conrad Gentzler,	do.	22 do.	
Henry Bott,	do.	do.	
Rynhard Botts,	do	do.	
John Runkett,	Berks,	do.	
Michael Keiser,	do.	do.	
Henry Sphon,	do.	do.	
Henry Zank,	Lancaster,	do.	
Martin Pattiker,	Berks,	do.	
Philip Breitenback,	Lancaster,	5 April,	1761
William Stoy,	do.	22 March,	1761
Jacob Grim,	Berks,	29 do.	
George Gansell,	do.	22 March.	
Henry Speecher,	York,	do.	
John Kuster,	Lancaster,	22 March,	1761
Mich'l Spengler,	do.	do.	
Nicholas Treber,	do.	26 March,	1761
John Treber,	do.	do.	
Henry Derr,	Berks,	7 April,	1761
John Huiand,	do.	do.	

Persons' names.	Of what place.	Sacramant, when taken	
John Shotter,	Lancaster,	3 April,	176
Mich'l Deny,	Chester,	15 March,	176
Mich'l Sifert,	do.	do.	
Michael Stout,	Berks,	1 April,	176
John Jacob Rabbold,	do.	6 do.	
Matthias Dornback,	do.	29 March,	176
Sebastian Rhutt,	do.	do.	
Henry Sanger,	do.	6 April,	176
Martin Bayer,	Berks,	5 do.	
Fred. Kern,	Northampton,	22 March,	176
John Made,	Berks,	29 do.	
Nicholas Runkett,	do.	do.	
George Englehard,	do.	7 April,	176
Martin Moore,	Berks,	29 March,	176
Jacob Heck,	do.	1 April,	176

And at the same Court the following persons, being Quakers or such who conscientiously scruple to take an oath, being also Foreigners, and having complied with the Terms required by the aforesaid act of Parliament, took and subscribed the Qualifications for them appointed by the same act of Parliament, &ca.

Persons' names.	Of what place.
Jacob Seigerist,	York County.
Ludwick Mohler,	Lancaster.
Martin Funk,	do.
Rudy Bollinger,	do.
Peter Heffley,	do.
John Bowman,	do.
Jacob Martin,	do.
John Senzeman,	do.
Jacob Keller.	do.
Valentine Hoffman,	do.
Peter Denny,	do.
Detrich Fannerstick,	do.
Conrad Bolthouse,	do.
Andrew Gear,	do.
Paul Gear,	do.
John Feegly,	do.
John Bougher,	do.
Martin Stover,	do.
Valentine Young,	Northampton.
Jno. Christ'r Hayne,	Lancaster.
Henry Mohler,	do.
Geo. Bless Renner,	do.
George Keller,	do.

Persons' names.	Of what place.	*If Moravians, Sacrament, when taken.*	
Jacob Mohler,	Lancaster.		
John Mather,	do.		
Christian Brenser,	do.		
Peter Brooker,	Berks.		
Valentine Hoff,	do.		
Jacob Stonmetz,	Philadelphia.		
John Lorey,	Berks.		
Peter Bryell,	do.		
Michael Andeas,	Lancaster.		
Jacob Rezer,	Berks.		
Philip Rezer,	do.		
Adam Spittlemyer,	do.		
Peter Wyland,	Lancaster.		
Jno. Feisser,	York,	21 March,	1761
Frantz Ludwick Berot,	do.	do.	
George Iglefritz,	do.	do.	
Jno. Beitzell,	do.	do.	
Bernhard Hewreisen,	do.	do.	
John Fishell,	do.	do.	
George Holler,	York.		
William Reel,	do.		
William Wirtz,	Lancaster.		
John Hover,	do.		
Christian Hartman,	do.		
Johannes Peter,	Philadelphia.		
Wilder Laudermeligh,	Lancaster.		
Jacob Mellinner,	do.		
Conrad Rush,	Philadelphia.		
John Mauyer,	Northampton.		
Valentine Young,	Berks.		
Adam Young,	do.		
Mich'l Small,	Philadelphia.		
Lazarus Weidner,	Berks.		
Dichius Weidner,	do.		
Philip Weinneimer,	Philadelphia.		
Lawrence Remich,	do.		
John Adam Kittering,	Lancaster,	19th March,	1761
Philip Trapp,	Northampton.		
Peter Tysse,	do.		
Hans Keller,	Berks.		
Jacob Lannius,	York,	21 March,	1761
Peter Huber,	Lancaster,	20 do.	
Jacob Shantz,	do.	do.	
Jacob Shertzer,	do.	do.	

Persons' names.	Of what place.
John Rupe,	Lancaster.
John Wingher,	do.
Jospeh Wingher,	do.
Francis Schunck,	Philadelphia.
Christian Kinsey,	Berks.
Adam Swartzback,	do.
Anthony Hamshaw,	do.
John Grove,	York.
Jacob Sheffer,	Berks.
Jacob Lewis,	Northampton.
Christian Eff,	Lancaster.
Peter Herple,	Berks.
Philip Cratzer,	Northampton.
Andreas Geiring,	do.
Conrad Miller,	Berks.
Baltzer Reem,	do.
Peter Beel,	do.
Henry Lowman,	Lancaster.
Abraham Paul,	do.
John Sneibly,	do.
Nicholas Huber,	do.
Andreas Izenhart,	Northampton.
Charles Shally,	Lancaster.
John Apple,	Northampton.
Henry Alshouse,	do.
Abraham Berlin,	do.
Frederick Saiger,	Lancaster.
Jno. Staily,	do.
Martin Apple,	Northampton.
Bernard Bare,	do.
Melcher Kneply,	do.
Christian Hoffert,	Philadelphia.
Henry Bush,	Northampton.
Henry Weaver,	do.
Gregorius Shultz,	do.
Andreas Warner,	Philadelphia.
Jno. Knagy,	Lancaster.
Jno. Vanlashy,	do.
Leonard Eckstine,	Philadelphia.
Elias Reed,	Berks.
Herny Sleighter,	Philadelphia.
Geo. Frederick,	do.
Christop'r Waggoner,	Northampton.
Crattius Larch,	do.
Jno. Melchor,	do.

Persons' names.	Of what place.
Moses Trable,	Philadelphia.
Jno. King,	do.
Geo. Starnher,	do.
Jacob Christian Gleim,	do.
Michael Stites,	do.

Certified by

WILLIAM ALLEN, Esq'r, *Chief Justice, &ca.*

The foregoing is a true and perfect List taken from the original Certificate under the hand of William Allen, Esq'r, remaining in my office.

RICHARD PETERS.

[And in like manner, in September Term following, to wit: On the tenth day of September, 1761, at the said Supream Court, before the said Judges, in pursuance of the aforesaid Act of Parliament, the following Persons:]

Foreigners' names.	County.	Sacrament, when taken.	
Albright Kochler,	Lancaster County,	26th July,	1761
Frederick Zeegle,	do.	do.	
Abraham Weidman,	do.	13 Sept.,	1761
George Miller,	do.	do.	
Jacob Schwaub,	do.	do.	
Martin Eichold,	do.	do.	
Christ Beechtel,	Berks,	17 August,	1761
Jacob Lehnherr,	Lancaster,	13 Sept.,	1761
Jacob Enck,	do.	do.	
Adam Jacobs,	do.	do.	
Geo. Mich'l Weiss,	do.	do.	
Jacob Bullinger,	do.	do.	
John Butser,	do.	20 Sept.,	1761
Thomas Kuhrr,	Berks,	17 August,	1761
Jacob Heidler,	do.	16 Sept.,	1761
Jno. Phil Schmid,	do.	do.	
Jno. Henry Goster,	do.	do.	
Jno. Henrick Byerle,	do.	do.	
Michael Laub,	Berks,	13 Sept.,	1761
Nich's Gorigher,	do.	do.	
Abraham Raiguel,	Lancaster,	do.	
Jno. Miller.	do.	do.	
Jacob Graff,	do.	do.	
Henry Gaebel,	do.	do.	
William Graff,	Berks,	18 Sept.,	1761
Wilhelm Ehrman,	do.	do.	
Joseph Berritt,	do.	do.	
Geo. Ernst Maurer,	do.	do.	

Foreigners' names.	County.	Sacrament, when taken.	
Erhard Rost,	Berks,	18 Sept.,	1761
Philip Sailor,	do.	do.	
Peter Knobb,	do.	20 Sept.,	1761
Henry Newkirk,	do.	do.	
Christp'r Smith,	Phiad'a,	do.	
Conrad Bab,	Berks,	14 Sept.,	1761
Geo. Neiss,	do.	do.	
Mich'l Glosser,	do.	do.	
Adam Apple,	do.	do.	
Jacob Mikely,	Northampton,	9 Aug't,	1761
Jacob Hottenstyn,	Lancaster,	20 Sept.,	1761
Nich. Winegardner,	do.	23 Aug't,	1761
Tobias Helsel,	York,	30 Aug't,	1761
Jacob Shoemaker,	Lancaster,	20 Sept.,	1761
Fred. Shingle,	do.	23 Aug't,	1761
Philip Umborne,	do.	do.	
Jacob Shaffner,	Lancaster,	23 Aug't,	1761
John Huber,	do.	do.	
Diederick Martin,	Berks,	20 Sept.,	1761
Sebastian Morgan,	do.	18 Sept.,	1761
Jno. Maurice Row.	Lancaster,	23 August,	1761
Christ'r Brytenhart,	Lancaster,	23 August,	1761
Nich Misser Smith,	do	do.	
Cha's Snyder,	do.	do.	
Christ'r Knurenshield,	do.	do.	
Frederick Martin,	do.	13 September,	1761
Martin Schredy,	do.	do.	
Christian Wallborn,	do.	do.	
Martin Battorff.	do.	do.	
Sebastian Krowser,	Berks,	16 Sept.,	1761
Conrad Brown,	do.	do.	
Sam. Shultz,	do.	do.	
Philip Weiss,	do.	do.	
Jacob Weld,	Lancaster,	20 September,	1761
Adam Bott,	York,	30 August,	1761
Peter Schaub,	Lancaster,	6 Sept.,	1761
Peter Feeser,	do.	do.	
Adam Krill,	do.	do.	
Nich. Weinhold,	do.	do.	
Marcus Eagle,	do.	do.	
George Hott,	do.	do.	
Will. Oldhouse,	Philadelphia,	13 September,	1761
John Henry Krause,	do.	20 Sept.,	1761
Frances Brosman,	Lancaster,	13 Sept.,	1761
Augustine Widder,	do.	20 Sept.,	1761

Foreigners' names.	County.	Sacrament, when taken.	
Charles Miller,	Lancaster,	20 Sept.,	1761
Mich'l Singhaas,	Philadelphia,	20 Sept.,	1761
Rudolph Fry,	do.	14 Sept.,	1761
Fred. Driesh,	do.	23 August,	1761
Adam Kowsman,	do.	do.	
Henry Klien,	do.	do.	
Johannes Kock,	Berks,	6 Sept.,	1761
Mich'l Kock,	do.	do.	
Martin Young,	do.	do.	
Jno. Peter Klinger,	do.	do.	
Martin Ege,	do.	do.	
John Dengler,	do.	do.	
Andreas Saltogeber,	Lancaster,	2 August,	1761
Matthias Strecher,	do.	30 August,	1761
Matth's Strecher, Jr.,	do.	6 Sept.,	1761
Philip Jacob Zinn,	York,	15 Sept.,	1761
Michael Bentz,	Lancaster,	30 August,	1761
Jacob Fry,	do.	23 Aug't,	1761
Jno. Adam Haushaller,	Berks,	6 Sept.,	1761
Nich. Gower.	do.	do.	
Jno. Godlit Bryninger,	do.	do.	
Henry Sclabach,	Lancaster,	do.	
Ludwick Wolfart,	Lancaster,	20 Sept.,	1761
Philip Maurer,	do.	do.	
Mich. Fischer,	Berks,	do.	
Jno. Casper Yager,	Philadelphia,	do.	
John Switzer,	Berks,	6 Sept.,	1761
John Henry Radin,	Lancaster,	26 July,	1761
George Marks,	Berks,	6 Sept.,	1761
Christ'r Embig,	Lancaster,	26 July,	1761
Henry Rineil,	do.	do.	
George Schupp,	do.	13 Sept.,	1761
Martin Yeck,	do.	30 Aug't,	1761
Jno. Martin Bryninger,	Berks,	6 Sept.,	1761
Philip Sulsback,	Philad'a,	20 Sept.,	1761
George Heist,	Berks,	6 Sept.,	1761
Detrick Sheffer,	do.	20 Sept.,	1761
Peter Rehm, Sen.,	Lancaster,	13 Sept.,	1761
Peter Rehm, Jun.,	do.	do.	
George Sheefer,	Berks,	20 Sept.,	1761
George Mees,	Lancaster,	13 Sept.,	1761
Adam Eckart,	Philad'a,	20 Sept.,	1761
Michael Bohr.	Lancaster,	30 August,	1761
William Stehr,	do.	do.	
Tillmar Shitz,	do.	13 Sept.,	1761

Foreigners' names.	County.	Sacrament, when taken.	
George Reinhard,	Lancaster,	13 Sept.,	1761
Jno. Wolfersberger,	do.	do.	
Jno. Tutwieler,	do.	do.	
Mich'l Rush, Sen.,	Berks,	6 Sept.,	1761
Mich'l Rush, Jun.,	do.	do.	
Anastasius Uhler,	Lancaster,	30 August,	1761
Wendal Hoyl,	do.	do.	
Adam Hullman,	do.	13 Sept.,	1761
Ludwick Mohn,	Berks,	18 Sept.,	1761
Jno. Newcomer,	do.	do.	
Chs. Ludwick Meclen-			
burgh,	Philad'a,	20 Sept.,	1761
Christ'r Curfiss,	do.	do.	
George Hefft,	Lancaster,	6 Sept.,	1761
Abraham Kern,	do.	do.	
John Snider,	Berks,	do.	
Henry Kitner,	Berks,	13 Sept.,	1761
Philip Staffer,	Lancaster,	6 Sept.,	1761
George Shaal,	Berks,	13 Sept.,	1761
Wendal Keemer,	Philad'a,	16 Sept.	
Michael Growl,	Berks,	21 Sept.,	1761
Lawrence Bitter,	Lancaster,	30 Sept.,	1761
John Deitz,	do.	do.	
Lehnhart Rubbert,	Berks,	18 Sept.,	1761
Jno. Phil. Klinger,	do.	6 Sept.,	1761
Alexander Klinger,	do.	do.	
Matthias Hinnelin,	do.	do.	
Jno. Geo. Eisinbiess,	do.	do.	
George Shadler,	do.	13 Sept.,	1761
Jno. Martin Fritz,	do.	do.	
Jno. Geo. Hafner,	Philad'a,	20 Sept.,	1761
George Reiss,	do.	do.	
Andrew Cammerel,	Lancaster,	23 August,	1761
Christian Gyger,	do.	do.	
Jno. Shryber,	do.	do.	
Jno. Kuster,	do.	23 August,	1761
Henry Mayer,	. do.	do.	
Mich'l Folemir,	Berks,	6 Sept.,	1761
Philip Nacks,	Berks,	18 Sept.,	1761
Jacob Yoacham,	Philad'a,	20 Sept.,	1761
Geo. Guyer,	Lancaster,	13 Sept.,	1761
Christop'r Boyer,	Berks,	6 Sept.,	1761
George Hoffer,	Lancaster,	20 Sept.,	1761
Adam New,	do.	2 August,	1761
Nicholas New,	do.	30 August,	1761

Foreigners' names.	County.	Sacrament, when taken.	
Conrad Rote,	Berks,	20 September,	1761
John Eberth,	do.	21 September,	1761
Andrew Ebbert,	do.	18 September,	1761
Valentine Vogt,	Philad'a,	16 September,	1761
Valentine Propst,	Berks,	20 Sept.,	1761
Nich. Schweiger,	do.	do.	
George Beeber,	do.	do.	
George Kutz,	do.	do.	
George Sell,	do.	do.	
Henry Alsback,	Berks,	16 September,	1761
Peter Knorr,	do.	do.	
Nicholas Yost,	do	do.	
Jno. Adam Neidig,	do.	do.	
Fred. Casemer Miller,	do.	do.	
Nicholas Heidsher,	do.	do.	
Michael Hessler,	do.	do.	
George Hoffman,	do.	do.	
Philip Spring,	do.	do.	
Conrad Glinder,	do.	do.	
Casper Snoble,	do.	13 Sept.,	1761
Ludwick Schui,	Lancaster,	13 September,	1761
Conrad Wohlfart,	do.	16 August,	1761
Jno. Gunckel,	Berks,	20 September,	1761
Conrad Hart,	do.	6 September,	1761
Frederick Barlet,	do.	do.	
Jno. Marks Rininger,	Philad'a,	do.	
Conrad Steer,	Bucks,	16 August,	1761
Martin Shabecker,	do.	do.	
Michael Yoh,	Philad'a,	do.	
Henry Gittleman,	do.	6 September,	1761
Jno. Jos. Roth,	do.	16 August,	1761
Philip Wentz,	do.	6 September,	1761
Henry Heist,	do.	13 August,	do.
Mich'l Gratz,	do.	do.	
John Riess,	Northampton,	13 Sept.,	1761
Lawrence Ficks,	Berks,	6 Sept.,	1761
Abraham Shriner,	Bucks,	13 Sept.,	1761
Henrick Engle,	Philad'a,	20 Sept.,	1761
Christian Sneeder,	Lancaster,	21 Sept.,	1761
Thomas Yerger,	Philad'a,	13 Sept.,	1761
Valentine Sherer,	do.	20 Sept.,	1761
Andrew Yerger,	do.	13 Sept.,	1761
Jno. Ruef Snyder,	Berks,	20 Sept.,	1761
Martin Bower,	Bucks,	30 August,	1761
George Gilbert,	Berks,	21 Sept.,	1761

Foreigners' names.	County.	Sacrament, when taken.	
Jacob Gieger,	Philad'a,	13 Sept.,	1761
Leonard Immel,	York,	30 August,	1761
Fred. Kreemer,	Berks,	13 Sept.,	1761
Jacob Dietrick,	do.	do.	
George Waldhawer,	Lancaster,	23 August,	1761
Christopher Wald-hawer,	do.	do.	
Fred Glass,	do.	30 August,	1761
Mich'l Propst,	Berks,	24 Septemb'r,	1761
Jno. Kistler,	do.	do.	
Simon Freest,	do.	do.	
Jacob Hoggabugh,	Berks,	24 September,	1761
Jacob Dreess,	do.	do.	
Chas. Kachlin,	Bucks,	30 August,	1761
Conrad Stighter,	Berks,	6 Sept.,	1761
Jacob Kiemil,	Northampton,	13 Septem'r,	1761
George Mich'l Koll,	Philadelp'a,	20 Sept.,	1761
Adam Koch,	Cumberland,	24 Sept.,	1761
Nich. Swartz,	Berks,	13 Septem'r,	1761
Geo. Eberhard,	Philad'a	22 Septem'r,	1761
Jacob Roth,	do.	do.	
Daniel Erhard,	do.	24 September,	1761
Jno. Christ'r Fred. Wolf,	do.	20 September,	1761
Jno. Dan. Maylander,	do.	do.	
Geo. Christ'r Reinhold,	do.	5 July,	1761
Jerem'h Barr,	Berks,	6 Sept.,	1761
Casper Tilling,	Lancaster,	16 August,	1761
John Bowse,	Bucks,	20 Sept..	1761
Peter Meesmer,	Northampton,	13 September,	1761
Geo. Adam Heilman,	Chester,	20 September.	1761
Geo. Christ'r Eberley,	Philad'a,	5 July,	1761
John Jacob Binder,	do.	20 September,	1761
Jno. Fred Uhland,	do.	do.	

And at the same Court the following Persons being Quakers. or such who conscientiously scruple to take an oath, being also Foreigners, and having complied with the Terms required by the aforesaid act of Parliament, took and subscribed the Qualifications for them appointed by the same act of Parliament, &ca. :

Foreigners' names.	Of what county.	If Moravians, Sacrament, when taken.
John Gruber,	Chester.	
Jacob Rohrer,	Lancaster.	
Mich. Bower,	York.	

Foreigners' names.	*Of what county.*	*If Moravians, Sacrament, when taken.*	
William Reeser,	Berks.		
John Miley,	Lancaster.		
Nich. Surface,	do.		
Henry Brunner,	do.		
Ulrick Supinger,	do.		
Christ'r Sullinger,	do.		
Christ'n Uplinger,	do.		
Jacob Lidert,	do.		
Ulrick Weetmore,	do.		
John Bender,	Lancaster,	29 August,	1761
Frederick Rautforin,	Lancaster.		
Cath'ne Levan (former-			
ly Quimore,)	Berks.		
Christ'n Brunesholtz,	Lancaster.		
Jacob Frutz,	do.		
Emanuel Brolliar.	do.		
Johannes Clineyenny,	Berks.		
Peter Assum,	Lancaster.		
Abram Smoutz,	do.		
Geo. Brendel,	Berks.	6 Septem'r,	1761
Simon Aigler,	do.	do.	
Mich. Lower,	do.	do	
John Bentz,	York.		
John Moyer,	Northampton.		
Jacob Dobler,	Lancaster.		
George Sysinger,	Berks.		
Bernard Ropost,	do.		
Martin Bouher,	Lancaster.		
Geo. Schweeter,	do.		
Barth'w Seeggrist,	do.		
John Carver,	Berks.		
Christian Luke,	do.		
Joseph Mishler,	do.		
Jacob Mishler,	do.		
Adam Rickabacker,	do.		
Philip Brindle,	Lancaster.		
John Rudy,	do.		
Philip Eckert,	do.		
John Shultz,	do.	13 September,	1761
Conrad Swartz,	do.		
Geo. Miley,	York.		
John Stouffer,	Lancaster.		
Christ'r Wither,	do.		
Barbara Ritter,	Berks.		

Foreigners' names.	Of what county.	If Moravians, Sacrament, when taken.	
Daniel Born,	Lancaster,	10 September,	1761
Bernhard Faber,	do.	do.	
Jacob Spikeler,	do.		
Adam Faber,	do.		
Philip Bake,	do.		
Jacob Gootz,	Berks.		
John Newcomat,	Lancaster.		
Matthias Seidler,	do.		
John Bideler,	Philadelphia.		
Jacob Speedler,	Lancaster.		
John Markle,	do.		
Dorst Thomas,	do.		
Abraham Bomper,	Northampton,	21 August,	1761
Andreas Schoute,	do.	do.	
John Lisher,	do.	do.	
Fred. Backle,	do.	do.	
Andreas Weber,	do.	do.	
Francis Grove,	York.		
John Amend,	do.		
Fred. Hoove,	Berks.		
Anthony Snyder,	Lancaster.		
Barbara Ritter,	Berks.		
Peter Ganter,	Lancaster.		
David Tressler,	do.		
Bernard Brodbeck,	do.		
Martin Pfatteger,	Berks.		
John Martin,	Philad'a.		
Jacob Kocknower,	Lancaster.		
Valentine Eckert,	Berks.		
George Trone,	York.		
Henry Bowman,	do.		
Phil. Henry Dahne,	Lancaster,	22 August,	1761
John Hickman,	do.		
Matthias Bysher,	York.		
Philip Bushung,	Lancaster.		
Adam Deafisback,	do.		
Jacob Rowlond,	do.		
Jno. Chr'n Guteyahr,	Lancaster,	29 August,	1761
Andrew Hoover,	Frederick, in Maryland.		
Jacob Kockanon,	Lancaster.		
Abraham Kurtz,	do.		
Christian Smoker,	do.		
Christian Rohrback,	do.		
Jacob Keentzey,	do.	6 September,	1761

Foreigners' names.	Of what county.	If Moravians, Sacrament, when taken.	
Jno. Heekendorn,	York,	9 September,	1761
Jacob Viest,	do.		
John Fishel,	Lancaster.		
Ludwick Shally,	Lancaster.		
Valentine Kaller,	do.		
Jno. Motezer,	Berks.		
Jacob Early,	do.		
John Keever,	Hunterdon in New Jersey.		
Henry Baker,	Philad'a.		

Certified by

WILLIAM ALLEN, Esq'r.,
Chief Justice, &ca.

The foregoing is a true and perfect List, taken from the original certificate, under the Hand of William Allen, Esqr., remaining in my office.

RICHARD PETERS.

Transmitted to the Board of Trade by Captain ——

———

[And in like manner, in April Term following, to wit: On the tenth and twelfth days of April, 1762, at the said Supream Court, before the said Judges, in pursuance of the afores'd Act of Parliament, the following Persons:]

Foreigners' names.	County.	Sacrament, when taken.	
Christian Moy,	Philadelphia,	9 April,	1762
Wemer Weitzel,	Berks,	21 March,	1762
Daniel Masserly,	York,	21 March,	1762
John Nicholas King,	do.	do.	
John Peter Wolfe,	do.	do.	
Lawrence David Rippell,	do.	do.	
Jno. Leonard Shedoran,	do.	do.	
Michael Zinser,	Philadelphia,	14 March,	1762
John Peter Goodling,	York,	21 March,	1762
John Nich's Schrain,	do.	do.	
John Wolff,	do.	do.	
John Backenstoose,	Lancaster,	21 July,	1762
Peter Lent,	York,	8 April,	1762
Frederick Weitzell,	Berks,	4 April,	1762
Peter Beer, Senior,	Lancaster,	21 Febr'y,	1762
Barnet Wolf,	do.	do.	
Frederick Youse,	York,	4 April,	1762
John Fockler,	do.	do.	
Andrew Rudesill,	do.	do.	
Ludwick Mayer,	do.	do.	

Foreigners' names.	County.	Sacrament, when taken.	
Michael Sommer,	York,	4 April,	1762
Wendall Laumeister,	do.	do.	
Conrad Maul,	Lancaster,	7 March,	1762
Yost Waggoner,	do.	4 April,	1762
Philip Graber,	do.	do.	
Philip Hoss,	do.	do.	
Henry Graber,	do.	do.	
Adam Roppert,	do.	do.	
Baltzer Shafer,	Lancaster,	21 February,	1762
Peter Reighter,	do.	do.	
John Huber,	York,	4 April,	1762
John Shauman,	do.	do.	
George Spanseiler,	do.	do.	
John Schoron,	York,	14 April,	1762
Ludewic Miller,	do.	do.	
Andreas Fucks,	Berks,	do.	
Jacob Deem,	do.	do.	
John Swartzhoupt,	do.	do.	
Andreas Schaber,	do.	do.	
Jacob Kuntz,	do.	do.	
George Burkhard,	Lancaster,	21 April,	1762
Valentine Weber,	do.	do.	
John Doll,	do	do.	
John Graff,	do.	do.	
Henry Bott,	do.	do.	
Philip Miller,	York,	4 April,	1762
Michael Long,	do.	do.	
John George Spahr,	York,	do.	
Jno. Casper Marberg,	Lancaster,	21 February,	1762
John Hoofnaigle,	do.	do.	
Abraham Caubal,	do.	do.	
Adam LeRoy,	do.	do.	
Henry Bergey,	Northampton,	4 April,	1762
Jacob Moor,	do.	do.	
Jacob Petre,	Bucks,	do.	
John Wirmley,	Lancaster,	7 March,	1762
Jacob Krowter,	do.	4 April,	1762
Lawrence Shrunck,	Berks,	1 April,	1762
Valentine Baumgartner,	do.	do.	
Peter Reti,	do.	do.	
Valentine Kayser,	do.	do.	
Uti Ritschart,	do.	do.	
Baltzer Zerch,	do.	do.	
Detrick Sole,	do.	4 April,	1762
Henry Sole,	do.	do.	

Foreigners' names,	County,	Sacrament, when	taken
Henry Fry,	Berks,	4 April,	1762
John Bast,	Berks,	do.	
George Sibert,	do.	do.	
John Wesner,	do.	do.	
Adam Hawker,	Lancaster,	do.	
Adam Oberley,	do.	do.	
Chas. Schaid,	do.	do.	
Jacob Schneizer,	do.	do.	
Philip Hoffman,	do.	do.	
Michael Dewald,	Berks,	do.	
Gerhard Will,	Berks,	4 April,	1762
Andrew Hagebuck,	do.	do.	
George Kishtler,	do.	do.	
Philip Miller,	Northampton,	4 April,	1762
Henry Lease,	Berks,	5 April,	1762
Henry Sheirer,	do.	do.	
Philip Henzel,	do.	do.	
Bastian Kreicher,	do.	do.	
Adam Lukembiel,	do.	do.	
Forst Kreicher,	do.	do.	
Casper Smit,	do.	do.	
David Alspack,	do.	do.	
David Brining,	do.	do.	
Jno. Fraunveller,	do.	do.	
Frederick Blatt,	do.	do.	
Frederick Lease,	do.	do.	
Hieronimus Proback,	Lancaster,	28 March,	1762
Christian Grove,	do.	do.	
Jno. Schnabel,	Berks,	21 March,	1762
Paul Lingel,	do.	do.	
Jno. Pontius,	Berks,	21 March,	1762
Michael Powser,	do.	4 April,	1762
Casper Hinckel,	do.	do.	
Valentine Urledick,	Berks,	4 April.	1762
Jno. Christop'r Neidlin,	do.	do.	
Fred. William Frick,	do.	do.	
Werner Stam,	do.	1 April,	1762
Adam Sontag,	do.	do.	
Jacob Fox,	do.	4 April,	1762
Jacob Stough,	do.	do.	
George Christian,	do.	do.	
Martin Cronmiller,	York,	do.	
Peter Peres,	do.	do.	
Philip Mayer,	Berks,	21 March,	1762
Detrick Meyer,	York,	do.	

24—VOL. II.

Foreigners' names.	County.	Sacrament, when taken.	
Andrew Schaub,	Lancaster,	9 April,	1762
Hans Ulrick Angst,	Philadelphia,	do.	
Henrick Conrad,	do.	do.	
Joseph Dinshirtz,	Lancaster,	7 March,	1762
Jacob Wertz,	Cumberland,	10 April,	1762
Leonard Sable,	York,	do.	
John Wolf,	Philadelphia,	10 March.	
Adam Protzman,	do.	do.	
Jno. Michael Shubert,	do.	14 March,	1762
Melchior Hay,	Northampton,	4 April,	1762
Jacob Prutzman,	do.	do.	
Geo. Tho's Heymber-ger,	Philadelphia,	10 April,	1762
Herman Atchey,	do.	9 April,	1762
Daniel Reynhard,	do.	do.	
Jacob Gobler,	do.	do.	
John Ederick.	do.	do.	
George Troutman,	Lancaster,	21 February,	1762
Jno. George Beck,	Philadelphia,	14 March,	1762
Jno. George Sauter,	do.	do.	
Jno. George Kugler,	do.	do.	
Geo. Adam Rockeber-ger,	Philadelphia,	14 March,	1762
Geo. Adam Pfister,	do.	do.	
Gallus Sleighter,	do.	10 April,	1762
Jno. Christian Læser,	do.	11 April,	1762
George Snæring,	do.	do.	
Henry Krips,	do.	do.	
Geo. Ludwick Meyer,	Lancaster,	7 March,	1762
Paul Weitzel,	do.	21 February,	1762
George Ernst Linden-berger,	Philadelphia,	11 April,	1762
Jno. George Herniess,	do.	do.	
William Stadleman,	do.	do.	
Jacob Korr,	do.	do.	
Baltzer Spitznagle,	do.	do.	
Baltzer Weig,	do.	do.	
Barbara Mehl,	do.	14 March,	1762
Jacob Hiltzheimer,	do.	29 Mar.,	1762
John Odenheimer,	do.	do.	

At the same Court the following Persons being Quakers, or such who conscientiously refuse to take an oath, being also Foreigners, and having complied with the terms required by the aforesaid act of Parliament, took and subscribed the Qualifications for them appointed by the same act of Parliament, &ca. :

Foreigners' names.	County.	If Moravians, Sacrament, when taken.	
Jacob Ecker,	Lancaster.		
John Francis Reimer,	do.		
Nicholas Burkhardt,	Philadelphia.		
Adam Camel,	do.		
Andrew Gelinger,	Lancaster.		
Henry Wert,	York.		
Jacob Bleck, of Frederick county, in Maryland.			
John Kramer,	Lancaster,	3d April,	1762
Frederick Weisel,	Bucks.		
John Artz,	Berks.		
John Crush,	Lancaster.		
George Everly,	do.		
Peter Mumma,	do.		
George Hoofney,	do.		
Jacob Stooner,	do.		
Martin Wesner,	Berks.		
Rosind Kirsten,	Berks.		
Henry Ulius,	York.		
Christopher Master,	Berks.		
Philip Boyer,	Philadelphia.		
Nathaniel Seidel,	Northampton,	13 March,	1762
Nich. Henry Eberhardt,	Lancaster,	do.	
Matthias Weiss,	Northampton,	13 March,	1762
Jacob Stambach,	York,	do.	
Anthony Kreber,	do.		
Martin Kryder,	Philadelphia.		
Conrad Rœsslie,	Northampton.		
Casper Wenk,	Berks.		
Jacob Fry,	Northampton.		
Valentine Ertell,	York.		
Conrad Detry,	Philadelphia.		
John Rode,	do.		
Frederick Fetzer,	do.		
Tobias Weber,	Philadelphia.		
John Sumer,	Philadelphia.		
George Piecus,	do.		

Certified by

WILLIAM ALLEN, Esquire,
Chief Justice, &c.

The foregoing is a true and perfect List from the Original Certificate under the Hand of William Allen, Esquire, remaining in my office.

JOSEPH SHIPPEN, Jr.,
Secretary.

Transmitted to the Board of Trade by the Carolina, Capt. Friends, the 16th November, 1763.

[And in like manner, in September term following, viz: On the twenty-fourth day of September, 1762, at the said Supream Court before the said Judges, in pursuance of the aforesaid Act of Parliament, the following persons, viz:[

Foreigners' names.	County.	Sacrament, when taken.	
Martin Schneider,	Lancaster,	September 19,	1762
John Honshire,	do.	Sept.	12, 1762
Philip Olinger,	do.	August	8, 1762
Jacob Hacker,	do.	do.	
George Glassbenner,	do.	do.	
Geo. Mich'l Balmir,	do.	do.	
Geo. Householder,	do.	do.	
Peter Shaaf,	do.	Sept.	12, 1762
Ludwick Lay,	Lancaster,	12 Sept.,	1762
John Peter Cugnet,	do.	do.	
Casper Senghaar,	do.	29 August,	1762
George Ehler,	do.	22 do.	
John Kann,	do.	12 Sept.,	1762
Benjamin Moses Clava, a Jew.			
George Petri,	Lancaster,	16 Sept.,	1762
Philip Bechtoe,	do.	do.	
Simon Wishong,	do.	do.	
Peter Lederman,	Lancaster,	21 Sept.,	1762
Martin Englibright,	York,	20 Sept.,	1762
Paul Gyer,	do.	do.	
Nicholas Ott,	do.	do.	
Simon Laibell,	Lancaster,	1 August,	1762
John Wall,	York,	19 Sept.,	1762
Michael Welsh,	do.	do.	
Godfried Kenig,	do.	do.	
Jacob Philip Kenig,	do.	do.	
Christ'r Rodermill,	do.	29 July,	1762
Michael Weber,	Lancaster,	1 August,	1762
Peter Schain,	Berks,	19 Sept.,	1762
George Ellinger,	Lancaster,	8 August,	1762
John Comfort,	York,	19 Sept.,	1762
Henry Smith,	do.	do.	

Foreigners' names.	County.	Sacrament, when taken.	
Henry Baum,	York,	19 Sept.,	1762
Andrew Comfort,	do.	do.	
John Hurback,	do.	do.	
Jacob Stence,	do.	19 Sept.,	1762
John Melford,	Chester,	19 Sept.,	1762
Casper Melford,	do.	do.	
John Kline,	Berks,	12 Sept.,	1762
Christian Schweetzer,	Lancaster,	16 Sept.,	1762
Andrew Clyne,	do.	22 August,	1762
Rudolph Spingler,	York,	19 Sept.,	1762
Jacob Stam,	do.	do.	
Bernard Spengler,	do.	do.	
George Zimmerman,	Berks,	do.	
Jacob Dubree,	do.	16 Sept.,	1762
John Reslvi,	Lancaster,	23 August,	1762
Baltzer Gaitz,	do.	do.	
Henry Ryledorfes,	Berks,	2 Sept.,	1762
John Weaver,	Lancaster,	12 Sept.,	1762
Henrick Nehroot,	Berks,	2 Sept.,	1762
John Hiem,	do.	8 Sept.,	1762
Daniel Smith,	do.	do.	
Bernard Wannemaker,	Northampton,	8 Sept.,	1762
Max Wannemaker,	do.	do.	
Jacob Gerhart,	Berks,	do.	
George Drum,	do.	do.	
John Philips,	do.	13 Sept.,	1762
Jacob Shuman,	do.	16 Sept.,	1762
John Philip Baker,	Lancaster,	12 Sept.,	1762
Martin Long,	Berks,	12 Sept.,	1762
George Rodebach,	do.	do.	
Jacob Artz,	do.	12 Sept.,	1762
Jacob Heck,	York,	20 Sept.,	1762
Andrew Smith,	do.	do.	
Peter Shriber,	do.	do.	
Nicholas Wild,	do.	19 Sept.,	1762
John Jacob Poh,	Berks,	2 Sept.,	1762
Werner Stouck,	do.	5 Sept.,	1762
John Miller,	do.	2 Sept.,	1762
Jacob Nagle,	do.	19 Sept.,	1762
Peter Lebengut,	do.	do.	
Ludwick Bender,	do.	do.	
Rowland Young,	do.	do.	
John Kehl,	do.	do.	
Conrad Keifsneider,	do.	do.	
Andrew Weiler,	do.	do.	

Foreigners' names.	County.	Sacrament, when taken.	
Adam Leibengut,	Philadelphia,	19 Sept.,	1762
Abraham Jorrigg,	Lancaster,	25 June,	1762
Jacob Kinser,	do.	23 August,	1762
Peter Rodebach,	Berks,	16 Sept.,	1762
Andrew Aulenbacker,	do.	do.	
Jacob Whitmer,	Lancaster,	19 Sept.,	1762
Henry Leinweeber,	do.	do.	
Stephen Hauk,	Berks,	do.	
Henry Anth'y Koenig,	do.	14 Sept.,	1762
Peter Klingman,	do.	2 Sept.,	1762
Martin Probst,	do.	do.	
Frederick Heese,	do.	do.	
Michael Zimmerman,	do.	18 July,	1762
Philip Ensminger,	do.	23 August,	1762
William Hesfer,	do.	do.	
Michael Nick,	Philadelphia,	23 September,	1762
Henry Peter,	York,	19 Sep't,	1762
Francis Kuntz,	Lancaster,	12 Sep't,	1762
Adam Kohn,	York,	19 Sep't,	1762
Casper Egly,	Berks,	5 Sep't,	1762
George Schram,	York,	19 Sep't,	1762
Peter Sahler,	do.	do.	
John Philip Seydig,	Philadelphia,	19 Sept.	
Henry Krauss,	do.	19 Sep't,	1762
Jacob Kopp,	do.	Sep't	12, 1762
Jacob Wist,	Berks,	Sep't	5, 1762
Ulrick Mohn,	do.	do.	
Mary Eliz. Endris,	Philadelphia,	Sep't	12, 1762
George Bernhardus,	Berks,	do.	
Peter Diehm,	do.	do.	
Nicholas Mateery,	do.	do.	
Nicholas Gotschall,	do.	do.	
Bernard Mans,	Lancaster,	Sep't	12, 1762
John Gaerber,	Berks,	Sep't	19, 1762
Jacob Fries,	Northampton,	do.	
Peter Fries.	do.	do.	
George Shiesler,	Berks,	do.	
John Myer,	Northampton,	5 Sep't,	1762
Lawrence Hersher,	York,	Sep't	19, 1762
John Miller,	Lancaster,	Sep't	17, 1762
Deitrick Thopf,	do.	Sep't	21, 1762
Veit Penner,	York,	Sep't	19, 1762
Philip Kohl,	Berks,	Sep't	5, 1762
John Neiss,	Bucks,	Sep't	14, 1762
Michael Shaffer,	Northampton,	Sep't	12, 1762

Foreigners' names.	County.	Sacrament, when taken.	
Henry Berger,	Berks,	Sep't	15, 1762
Nicholas Pontius,	do.	do.	
Philip Rode,	do.	do.	
Henry Sleigh,	do.	5 Sep't,	1762
Frederick Herner,	do.	do.	
Bernard Leveitzig,	Berks,	24 August,	1762
George Angstat,	do.	do.	
George Born,	do.	Sep't	6, 1762
Embrick Monmemaker,	Philadelphia,	Sep't	14, 1762
Peter Schilp,	Northampton,	Sep't	12, 1762
Conrad Fucks,	do.	do.	
John Shultz,	York,	Sep't	19, 1762
Jacob Shultz,	do.	do.	
Jacob Welsh,	do.	do.	
Nicholas Schavas,	do.	do.	
Adam Schmaal,	do.	do.	
Martin Gryder,	Kent,	15 Aug't,	1762
John Emig,	York,	19 Sep't,	1762
Godfrey Fry,	do.	do.	
George Basbon,	Philadelphia,	19 Septemb'r,	1762
Valentine Miller,	do.	do.	
Lawrence Reber,	Berks,	12 Sept.,	1762
George Miller,	do.	do.	
Henry Miller,	do.	do.	
Adam Bower,	do.	do.	
Adam Brosst,	Northampton,	9 Sept.,	1762
Bernard Smith,	do.	do.	
John Richart,	Philadelphia,	19 Sept.,	1762
John Niep,	Lancaster,	1 August,	1762
Jacob Grimm,	Northampton,	19 Sept.,	1762
Henry Kockenbach,	do.	do.	
Ludwick Huke,	Bucks,	21 Sept.,	1762
Leonard Burkheimer,	Philadelphia,	1 August,	1762
Henry Rocky,	Lancaster,	do.	
Felix Bachman,	do.	do.	
Nich's Seydall,	Berks,	19 Sept.,	1762
Jacob Eckell,	Philadelphia,	do.	
Frederick Hummell,	Lancaster,	5 Sept.,	1762
Peter Schug,	Philadelphia,	12 Sept.,	1762
John Gantz,	do.	do.	
Theophilus Engeland,	Lancaster,	5 Sept.,	1762
Paul Schwanger,	Philadelphia,	12 Sept.,	1762
Philip Schoenberger,	do.	19 Sept.,	1762
Valentine Uhler,	Northampton,	27 June,	1762
William Fulbright,	do.	do.	

Foreigners' names.	County.	Sacrament, when taken·	
John Michael Kock,	Northampton,	27 June,	1762
George Keen,	do.	do.	
John William Kell,	do.	do.	
Sebastian Kayser,	do.	do.	
Frederick Weiss,	Lancaster,	1 August,	1762
Peter March,	Berks,	19 Sept.,	1762
John Deal,	do,	29 Sept.,	1762
Jacob Bechtel,	do.	5 Sept.,	1762
Mich'l Greyshir,	do.	15 August,	1762
George May,	do.	do.	
Christ'r Maurer,	Philadelphia,	29 August,	1762
Michael Plutner,	do	1 August,	1762

Benjamin Moses Clava, before named, being a Jew, was Qualified and Subscribed the Declaration, &ca., according to ye directions of the Act of the 13 of King George the second aforementioned.

At the same Court the following persons, being Quakers, or such who conscientiously scruple to take an oath, being also foreigners & having complied with the Terms required by the aforesaid act of Parliament, took and subscribed the Qualifications for them appointed by the same act of Parliament, &ca:

Foreigners' names.	County.	Moravians, time of Taking ye Sacram't.	
George Stayley,	Lancaster.		
John Deer,	do.		
Jacob Seyler,	do.		
Ulrick Reighart,	do.		
Jacob Henning,	do.		
Henry Waggoner,	do.		
Isaiah Whitehead,	do.		
Adam Falker,	do.		
Eronimus Miller,	do.		
John Lowtherman,	do.		
Jacob Kitz,	do.		
Barbara Messersmidt,	Berks.		
Hans Hoppiker,	Lancaster.		
Charles Ullendorf,	Northampton.		
John George Geinert,	do.	13 August,	1762
Christ'r Fred. Oerter,	do.	13 August,	1762
Benedict Spitzfarden,	Lancaster.		
Peter Kingrick,	do.		
John Wilhelm Foulke,	Berks.		
Matthias Kulp,	do.		
Adam Helm,	Philadelphia,	July 31,	1762
Bernard Strauss,	Northampton.		

Foreigners' names.	County.	Moravians, time of Taking ye Sacram't.	
Adam Hoff,	York,	18 Sept.,	1762
Sibeld Tetern,	Bucks.		
Marcus Haines,	York.		
Jacob Henrick,	do.		
Christian Gayman,	Berks.		
Bernard Rapp,	Philadelphia.		
Jacob Frick,	Bucks..		
Jacob Peterman,	Philadelphia.		
Jacob Uhlum,	do.		
Jno. Matthew Otto,	Northampton,	13 August,	1762
Mathew Schropp,	do.	8 Sept.,	1762
Casper Devilsbit,	Frederick co'y, Maryland.		
Henry Mann,	Philadelphia.		
Certified by			

WILLIAM ALLEN, Esquire,
Chief Justice, &ca.

The foregoing is a true and perfect List, from the original Certificate under the Hand of William Allen, Esqr., remaining in my office.

JOSEPH SHIPPEN, Jr.,
Secretary.

Transmitted to the Board of Trade by the Carolina, Cap't Friend, 16th November, 1763.

[At a Supream Court held at Philadelphia, before William Allen and William Coleman, Esquires, Judges of the said Court, the eleventh Day of April, in the year of our Lord one thousand seven hundred & sixty-three, Between the Hours of nine & twelve of the Clock in the Forenoon of the same Day, the following Persons being Foreigners:]

Berks County.

Jurors' names.	Township.	Sacrament, when taken.	
Philip Nagel,	Reading,	April 3d,	1763
Ulrick Nodle,	do.	do.	
Michael Shecktell,	do.	do.	
Nicholas Tik,	do.	do.	
Andreas Fickthorn,	do.	do.	
John Mahrigen,	do.	do.	
Cathrina Kendel,	do.	do.	
Peter Smidt,	Heidleberg,	do.	
Leonard Spear,	Worcester,	do.	
Nicholas Slickting,	Reading,	do.	
Johannes Kurtz,	do.	do.	

Jurors' names.	Township.	Sacrament, when taken.	
Henry Haeffner,	Richmond,	April 3d,	1763
David Kamp,	do.	do.	
Melchior Fritz,	do.	do.	
Jeremiah Zimmer,	Brecknock,	do.	
Michael Frankhauser,	do.	do.	
Daniel Hoffman,	Reading,	do.	
Thomas Deem,	do.	do.	
John Christopher Lehman,	do.	do.	
Jacob Rossell,	Tolpohocken,	do.	
Jacob Miller,	do.	do.	
Peter Liess,	do.	do.	
Johan Hess,	do.	do.	
Henry Kremler,	Reading,	do.	
Johannes Sassamanhause,	Greenwich,	do.	
Peter Grienwald,	Richmond,	do.	
Henry Ardelle,	do.	do.	
George Kreemer,	Greenwick,	March 3d,	1763
Jacob Lewegood,	Tolpohocken,	April 3d,	1763
Godfried Kirker,	Heidelberg,	do.	
Henrick Eckhard,	Reading,	do.	
Jacob Fischer,	do.	do.	
Peter Flick,	Heidelberg,	Febr'y 13th,	1763
John Nicholas Strasser,	Albany,	April 11th,	1763
Peter Kruger,	Tulpehocken,	April 3d,	1763

Bucks County.

Philip Liester,	Rockland,	April 3d,	1763
Jacob Nonnemaker,	Hill Town,	do.	
John George Ott,	Bristol,	do.	
John Paul Boosse,	do.	do.	

Lancaster County.

Henry Maurer,	Lancaster,	April 3d,	1763
Balthasar Federfaaff,	Manhiem,	do.	
Wilpert Camper,	Lancaster,	do.	
Henry Rung,	do.	do.	
John Michael Becker,	Heidelberg,	do.	
Wilhelm Hoster,	do.	do.	
Balthasar Derter,	do.	do.	

Northampton County.

Eberhard Smith,	Weiseberg,	March 31st,	1763
Philip Wiedman,	Lynn,	do.	
Philip Shueman,	do.	April 5th,	1763

Jurors' names.	Township.	Sacrament, when taken.	
Henry Oswald,	Lynn,	April 5th,	1763
Simon Peter Scholl,	do.	March 31st,	1763
Leonard Frietshy,	Lower Saucon,	April 3d,	1763
William Albert,	Salisburg,	do.	
Sebastian Truckenmiller,	Upper Milford,	April 4th,	1763
Frederick Kammerer,	Macungy,	March 27th,	1763

Philadelphia County.

Michael Schlatter,	Springfield,	April 3d,	1763
George Adam Leopold,	City of Philad'a,	do.	
Balthasar Stienfurt,	do.	do.	
John Andrew Myer,	do.	do.	
John Martin Row,	do.	do.	
Henry Henkey,	do.	do.	
John Truckenmiller,	do	do.	
Arnd Rose,	do.	do.	
John Yahn,	New Hannover,	do.	
Baltzer Filler,	Frederick,	April 7th,	1763
John Lamparder,	Northern Liberties,	April 3d,	1763
Gregory Ritchy,	Whitemarsh,	do.	
John Kuhn,	City of Philad'a,	do.	
Peter Draiss,	do.	April 7th,	1763
Leonard Kesler,	do.	do.	
Jacob Frantz,	do.	April 3d,	1763
John Riely,	do.	do.	
Henry Stienmetz,	do.	do.	
John Henry Fisher,	Frankford,	do.	
Rudolph Neff,	Northern Liberties,	do.	
Jacob Neff,	Oxford,	do.	
Michael Kirman,	Northern Liberties,	do.	
John Ernst Mangen,	do.	do.	
Christopher Ludwig,	Philadelphia,	do.	
George Philip Weissman,	do.	do.	
John Daniel Mauty,	do.	do.	
Martin Walter,	Northern Liberties,	April 8th.	1763
Jacob Ehrard,	do.	April 3d,	1763
Adam Heise,	do.	do.	
Valentine Hagener,	City of Philadelphia,	do.	
John Frederick Teetz,	do.	do.	
George Peter Kockendoffer,	do.	do.	
Ludwick Spamagle,	Whitemarsh,	do.	
Christopher Pechin,	City of Philad'a,	do.	

Jurors' names.	Township.	Sacrament, when taken.	
Bernard Sherer,	Whitpain,	April 4th,	1763
Valentine Sherer,	do.	do.	
Jacob Benner,	Worcester,	do.	
Michael Reiffshnieder,	Dublin,	April 3d,	1763
John Fry,	Philadelphia,	do.	
Philip Filman,	Upper Salford,	do.	
Leonard Shneider,	do.	do.	
Christopher Gyser,	Marlborough,	do.	
Henry Bombarger,	Upper Salford,	do.	
Casper Hinterlicter,	Marlborough,	do.	
Mattheus Hinterlicter,	do.	do.	
John Alt,	do.	do.	
Matthew Landenberger,	City of Philadelphia,	April 11th,	1763
Hilarius Beker,	Germantown,	do.	
Matthias Smith,	Upper Dublin,	do.	
Frederick Knapp,	Springfield,	do.	
John Unruh,	Bristol,	April 3d,	1763
Jacob Kuns,	Springfield,	do.	
Felix Dutwyler,	do.	do.	
Abraham Wakerley,	do.	do.	
Andrew Highberger,	do.	do.	
Adam Hoffman,	North-Wales,	April 10th,	1763
Henry Kress,	Germantown,	April 3d,	1763
John Godfried Tule,	Northern Liberties,	do.	
Charles Witterhold,	Germantown,	do.	
Frederick Becking,	Lower Merrion,	do.	
Peter Stierwald,	Northern Liberties,	do.	
Andrew Erdman Leinau,	Philadelphia,	do.	

York County.

Andreas Shwartz,	Strasburg,	April 4th,	1763
Henry Walder,	do.	April 3d,	1763
Casper Glattsfelder,	Codorus,	do.	
Jacob Kern,	York,	do.	
Conrad Laudenbough,	do.	do.	
John Jacob Rhien,	Strasburg,	do.	
Jacob Walter,	Codorus,	do.	
Frederick Fishell,	do.	do.	
Philip Venus,	York,	April 4th,	1763
Philip Weber,	do.	April 3d,	1763
Henry Spengler,	do.	do.	
Peter Frett,	Windsor,	do.	
Adam Powlus,	do.	do.	
John Crone,	do.	do.	

Jurors' names.	*Township.*	*Sacrament, when taken.*
Michael Powlus,	Windsor,	April 3d, 1763
Nicholas Firestone,	Paradise,	do.
Andrew Frederick,	York,	do.

Frederick Co'ty, In Maryland.

Paul Cruss,	Frederick,	April 3d, 1763

Jurors' names.	*Township.*	*County.*	
Myer Josephson,	Reading,	Berks,	A Jew.
Lyon Nathan,	do.	do.	do.
Barnard Grats,	Philadelphia,	Philadelphia,	do.
Isaac Levy,	do.	do.	do.

The four Persons last aforenamed, being Jews, were qualified & subscribed the Declarations &ca., according to the Directions of the Act of the thirteenth of King George the second before mentioned. And the Persons hereafter named, being Foreigners, & of the People called Quakers & other Protestants, who conscientiously scruple the taking of an Oath, severally took the Affirmations, & made & subscribed the Declarations, according to the Directions of the same Act, entitled "an Act "for naturalizing such foreign Protestants, & others therein "mentioned, as are settled or shall settle in any of his Majesty's "Colonies in America," and of an Act of General Assembly of the Province of Pennsylvania, made in the year of our Lord one-thousand seven hundred and forty-two.

EDW. SHIPPEN, JR., *prot.*

Affirmers' names.	*Township.*	*County.*
Jacob Longenacre,	Coventry,	Chester.
Susannah Longenacre,	do.	do.
Anna Andrews,	Towamensing,	Philadelphia.
Adam Evey,	Philadelphia,	do. [Maryland.
Simbright Helsell,	Langenhose,	Frederick Co'ty, In
Frederick Sholeberger,	Greenwich,	Berks.
George Richwin,	Upper Dublin,	Philadelphia
Frederick Sallady,	Earl,	Lancaster.
Valentine Shamback,	New Providence,	Philadelphia.
William Busler,	Windsor,	Berks.
Philip Surface,	Philadelphia,	Philadelphia.
John Tzyle,	Lancaster,	Lancaster.
John Baker,	Plymouth,	do.
Simon Heller,	Lower Saucon,	Northampton.
Daniel Heller,	do.	do.
Ludwick Heller,	do.	do.
Henry Miller,	Mount Bethel,	do.

Affirmers' names.	Township.	County.	Moravians, time of their having taken the Sacrament.
George Martin,	Charlestown,	Chester.	
John Ellick,	City of Philad'a,	Philadelphia.	
Stephen Goodman,	Lower Merrion,	do.	
Christopher Mason,	Whitemarsh,	do.	
Charles Hay,	Bristol,	do.	
John Styer,	Hunterdon, In New Jersey.		
John Spore,	Lancaster,	Lancaster, April 1, 1763	

[At a Supream Court held at Philadelphia, before Lawrence Growdon and Willam Coleman, Esquires, Judges of the said Court, the twenty-fourth Day of September, in the Year of our Lord one thousand seven hundred and sixty-three, between the Hours of nine and twelve the Clock of in the forenoon of the same day, the following subscribing persons being foreigners:]

Philadelphia County.

Foreigners' names.	Township.	Sacrament, when taken.	
Philip Hall,	Philadelphia,	18th Sep'r,	176?
John Geetz,	do.	22d Sep'r,	176?
Jacob Reno,	do.	18th Sep'r,	176?
Michael Zeh,	do.	do.	
Andrew Heims,	do.	do.	
Leonard Miller,	Marlborough,	20th Sep'r,	176?
John Rupp,	Philadelphia,	23d Sep'r,	176?
Jacob Bernhard,	Limerick,	22d Sep'r,	176?
Michael Frederick,	Douglass,	21st Aug't,	176?
Michael Weidman,	do.	do.	
Arnd. Kurtz,	Limerick,	do.	
Michael Kurtz,	New Hannover,	do.	
Peter Gabel,	do.	do.	
John Mecklein,	do.	do.	
Philip Zeegler,	Upper Salford,	18th Sep'r,	176
Solomon Ruckstool,	do.	11th do	
John Faust,	do.	do.	
Ulrick Hurtzell,	do.	do.	
Philip Staug,	Lower Salford,	do.	
Frederick Keeler,	Worcester,	21st Aug't,	176
Peter Krowt,	do.	do.	
Conrad Fleck,	Northern Liberties,	4th Sep'r,	176
Frederick Groh,	Lower Merion,	11th Sep'r,	176
Henry Schmidt, Sen'r,	Frederick,	24th do.	
Henry Schmidt, jun'r,	Upper Hannover,	do.	
Jacob Duerr,	do.	do.	
John Beltz,	Passyunk,	23d Sep r,	176

Berks County.

Foreignors' name.	Township.	Sacrament, when taken	
Jacob Looss,	Windsor,	11th Sep'r,	1763
Balthazar Kleber,	Reading,	18th Sep'r,	1763
Jacob Fry,	Brecknock,	11th Sep'r,	1763
Jacob Crowl,	Reading,	18th Sep'r,	1763
John George Wunder,	do.	do.	
John George Huesung,	Brecknock,	22d Sep'r,	1763
John Shrict,	Cumru,	11th Sep'r,	1763
Philip Jacob Foesig,	Reading,	do.	
Jacob Walter,	Tulpehockin,	17th July,	1763
Nicholas Godschall,	Greenwich,	4th Sep'r,	1763

Bucks County.

Christian Steer,	Upper Milford,	18th Sep'r,	1763
Conrad Stenger,	Rockhill,	23d Sep'r,	1763
Philip Wonsidler,	Lower Milford,	14th Aug't,	1763

York County.

David Schaefer,	Shrewsbury,	18th Sep'r,	1763
Charles Dehl,	do.	do.	
John Meyer,	do.	do.	
Nicholas Schouster,	do.	11th Sep'r,	1763
Henry Eberhard,	Manchester,	23d Sep'r,	1763
Anthony Wolf,	do.	21st Aug't,	1763
Andrew Weir,	do.	do.	
Philip Gentzler,	York,	do.	
Erasmus Holtzapfel,	Manchester,	do.	
Martin Harry,	do.	do.	
George Liewenstien,	do.	do.	
Valentine Hamme,	Paradise,	do.	
Philip Lau,	Manchester,	4th Sep'r,	1763
Theobald Shallas,	Mount Pleasant,	do.	

Lancaster County.

Tobias Plieger,	Lancaster,	4th Sep'r,	1763
Joseph Long,	do.	do.	
John Brown,	do.	do.	
Philip Ohleweyler,	Mannor,	do.	
Yodocus Dobeler,	Lancaster,	do.	
John Hoffman,	do.	28th Aug't,	1763
Peter Ish,	do.	do.	
Abraham le'Roy,	do.	do.	
John Peter le'Roy,	do.	do.	
Michael Boltz,	Lebanon,	14th Aug't,	1763
Nicholas Haine,	Cocalico,	11th Sep'r,	1763
Casper Pfister,	Lampeter,	19th Aug't,	1763

Foreigners' names.	Township.	Sacrament, when taken.	
George Frederick,	Earl,	14th Sep'r,	1763
Frederick Lesser,	Cocalico,	21st Aug't,	1763

Northampton County.

Christian Reyner,	Upper Milford,	14th Aug't,	1763
Jacob Seecher,	do.	do.	

Chester County.

Peter Pechin,	Haverford,	25th Aug't,	1763

[The Persons hereafter named, being Foreigners, and of the People called Quakers, and other Protestants, who conscientiously scruple to take an Oath, severally took the Affirmations & made the Declarations according to the Directions of an Act of the thirteenth Year of King George the second, entitled "an Act for naturalizing such foreign Protestants and others therein mentioned as are settled or shall settle in any of his majesty's Colonies in America," and of an Act of General Assembly of the Province of Pennsylvania, made in the Year of our Lord one thousand seven hundred and forty-two :]

York County.

Foreigners' names.	Township.	Moravians, Sacrament, when taken	
Julius Brookhart,	Helm.		
Jacob Salback,	Berwick.		
Henry Wealer,	Paradise.		
Martin Binder,	York.		

Berks County.

Geoge Pearshler,	Oley.		
Valentine Fry.	Heidleberg,	11th Sep'r,	176
Jacob Cumerah,	Maxatawny.		
John Roadarmill,	Richmond.		

Lancaster County.

Henry Frank,	Berwick.		
Christian Stover,	Lampeter.		
Andrew Weiberick,	Lancaster,	3d Sep'r,	17(

West New Jersey.

Peter Overshield,	Kingwood.		

Philadelphia County.

Conrad Vanderwait,	North'n Liberties.		
Andrew Paul,	Limerick.		

Foreigners' names.	Township.
Joseph Piffer,	Springfield.
Jacob Carter,	do.
Philip Helzell,	Philadelphia.

Northampton County.

Jacob Hoobler,	Blanfield.

[At a Supreme Court held at Philadelphia, for the Province of Pennsylvania, Before William Coleman & Alexander Stedman, Esquires, two of the Judges of the said Court the tenth and twenty-third Days of April, in the year of our Lord one thousand seven hundred and sixty-four, Between the Hours of Nine and Twelve of the Clock in the Forenoon of the same day, the following subscribing Persons being Foreigners:]

Philadelphia County.

Foreigners' names.	Township.	Sacrament, when taken.	
Conrad Maag,	Philadelphia,	April	6th, 1764
Jacob Kaiser,	do.	do.	
George David Sickel,	do.	March	11th, 1764
John Martin Rees,	do.	do.	
George Walker,	do.	do.	
Nicholas Forsberg,	do.	March	11th, 1764
Jacob Tasht,	Marlborough,	March	23d, 1764
John Adam Hillegas,	Upper Hanover,	March	25th, 1764
John Michael Piper,	Philadelphia,	March	11th, 1764
Jacob Fuckerodt,	Oxford,	do.	
Peter Swartz,	Philadelphia,	April	11th, 1764
Adam Erben,	do.	April	8th, 1764
Michael Faucks,	do.	March	11th, 1764
Nicholas Jacob,	do.	do.	
Paul Moser,	New Hanover,	April	8th, 1764
Andreas Yeager,	do.	do.	
Bastian Moser,	Hanover,	April	10th, 1764
George Fuckerodt,	Oxford,	March	11th, 1764
John Philip de Haas,	Philadelphia,	April	22d, 1764

York County.

Jacob Lydie,	Codorus,	April	4th, 1764
Ulrick Hess,	Strasburg,	do.	
Martin Fry,	do.	March	25th, 1764
Gerrard Steegler,	do.	do.	
Mathias Alber,	Cocalico,	do.	
Abraham Stone.	do.	do.	
Nicholas Hoffman,	Dover,	April	1st, 1764

25—VOL. II.

Foreigners' names.	*Township.*	*Sacrament, when taken.*	
George Stough,	Dover,	April	1st, 1764
Frederick Stough,	do.	do.	
Adam Deel,	do.	do.	
George Deel,	do.	do.	
Frederick Kuhn,	York,	do.	
Killian Bebinger,	Roseborough,	April	4th, 1764
Frederick Reemer,	Codorus,	do.	
John Jacob Vogt,	Paradise,	April	11th, 1764
Leonard Gennevine,	Manheim,	April	10th. 1764
Cornad Keefaber,	do.	do.	

Berks County.

George Herhold,	Heidelberg,	April	6th, 1764
Jacob Erb,	do.	do.	
Mary Erb,	do.	do.	
Benedict Kebner,	Bern,	Feb'ry	26th, 1764
Henry Bollinger,	Long Swamp,	April	8th, 1764
Christian Rickstine,	Maiden Creek,	March	29th, 1764
Valentine Reintzel,	Tulpehocken,	April	1st, 1764
Charles Hei,	do.	do.	
George Boltz,	do.	do.	
Jacob Meenich,	Bethel,	do.	
John Rauensauner,	Rockland,	April	8th, 1764

Lancaster County.

Christian Voght,	Lancaster,	April	1st, 1764
Michael Bowsman,	do.	April	5th, 1764
Philip Albert,	Hempfield,	March	4th, 1764
Benjamin Lessly,	Brecknock,	March	18th, 1764

Bucks County.

Jacob Huber,	Rockhill,	April	1st, 1764
Conrad Kother,	Hilltown,	April	8th, 1764
Felix Ley,	Rockhill,	April	1st, 1764
Caspar Naglee,	Bedminster,	do.	
George Bisch,	Haycock,	April	8th, 1764
Michael Yost,	Bedminster,	do.	
John George Lowness,	Cushahoppen,	April	6th, 176

Northampton County.

Philip Brescher,	Macungy,	March	25th, 176
Jacob Wagner,	do.	do.	
Detrick Youmer,	do.	do.	
Matthew Ludwick,	do.	do.	
Frederick Shoemaker,	Upper Milford,	April	2d, 176
Adam Shoemaker,	do.	do.	
John Peter Miller,	do.	April	3d, 176
Myer Hart,	Easton, (a Jew.)		

The last mentioned Person, vizt: Myer Hart, being a Jew, was qualified and subscribed the Declarations, &c., according to the Directions of the aforesaid Act of the thirteenth of King George the Second.

Persons' names.	Of what place.	Sacrament, when taken.
John Schaffer,	Amwell, Hunterdon co., W. New Jersey, March	25th, 1764

The persons hereafter named being Foreigners, and of the people called Quakers and other Protestants who conscientiously scruple to take an Oath, severally took the affirmation & made & repeated the Declaration according to the Directions of the Act of the thirteenth of King Geroge the Second, entitled "an Act for Naturalizing such Foreign Protestants & others therein mentioned, as are settled or shall settle in any of his Majesty's Colonies in America," and of an Act of General Assembly of the Province of Pennsylvania, made in the year of our Lord one thousand seven hundred and forty-two.

York County.

Foreigners' names.	Township.	Sacrament, when taken by Moravians.
Isaac Stohler,	Manchester.	
Martin Myer,	Strasburg.	
George Conrad,	Pardise.	
John Conrad Knight,	Conawawga.	
Michael Burkey,	York.	
Herman Miller,	do.	
Herman Fitiar,	Reading.	

Lancaster County.

Jacob Stigleman,	Lancaster,	Feb'ry	25th, 1764
Andrew Horn,	Warwick,	March	17th, 1764
John Cline,	do.		

Berks County.

George Meintzer,	Robeson.
Henry Seitenbender,	Cumru.
Daniel Bussart,	do.
Casper Strabb,	Alsace.
Jacob Pliler,	do.
Philip Peter Scholl,	Maxatawny.

Northampton County.

John Musch,	Easton.		
David Zeisberger,	Bethlehem,	April	9th, 1764
John Jacob Schmick,	do.	March	24th, 1764
Daniel Kliest,	do.	March	10, 1764
John Adam Horsfield,	do.	do.	
Philip Sneider,	Lower Saucon.		

Philadelphia County.

Foreigners' names.	Township.	Sacrament, when taken by Moravians.
Jacob Helm,	Providence.	
John Hartman Haas,	do.	
John Behm,	North Wales.	
Nicholas Hazlebach,	Germantown.	
Daniel Rice,	Darby.	
William Long,	New Providence.	
Anthony Stiemer,	Germantown.	

New Jersey.

Daniel Pfeiffer,	Amwell,	Hunterdon, in Wes New Jersey.
Peter Miers,	do.	do.
Christop'er Lowbougher,	do.	do.

Bucks County.

Barnard Wintringor,	Hilltown.
Samuel Koffman,	Lower Milford.

[At a Supream Court held at Philadelphia, before William Allen, William Coleman and Alexander Stedman, Esquires Judges of the said Court, the twenty-fourth and twenty-fifth days of September, in the Year of our Lord one thousand seven hundred and sixty-four, between the Hours of nine and twelve of the clock in the Forenoon of the same days, the following persons being Foreigners:]

Philadelphia County.

Foreigners' names.	Township.	Sacrament, when taken	
John Fritz,	Southwark,	Sep'r	9th, 176
Michael Hetzell,	North'n Lib'ties,	do.	
Christian Bick,	Philad'a,	do.	
Jacob Boythyman,	North'n Lib'ties,	do.	
Jacob Wirking,	Philad'a,	do.	
Andrew Pertsch,	do.	do.	
George Knairr,	do.	do.	
John Nixley,	do.	do.	
Jacob Greiner,	do.	do.	
Jacob Frank,	Germantown,	Sep'r	8th, 17(
John Moyer,	Douglass,	Sep'r	21st, 17(
John Tzoller,	Hannover,	do.	
George Adam Egold,	do.	do.	
Martin Daggenbach,	do.	Sep'r	23d, 17(
John Schainer,	Douglass,	do.	
Paul Faiger,	Plymouth,	do.	

Foreigners' names.	Township.	Sacrament, when taken.	
Wilhelm Hildner,	Whitemarsh,	Sep'r	23d, 1764
Henry Kreyer,	Abington,	do.	
Jacob Houk,	Frederic,	do.	
Peter Hollebush,	do.	do.	
Christian Hollebush,	do.	do.	
Frederic May,	Upper Salford,	do.	
John Zoller,	Upper Hannover,	do.	
Philip Rowk,	do.	do.	
George, Lesher,	Passyunk,	Sep'r	9th, 1764
Godlieb Kriesinger,	Germantown,	Sep'r	23d, 1764
Conrad Schutz,	Upper Hannover,	Sep'r	16th, 1764
John Metzler,	Germantown,	Sep'r	9th, 1764
Rinehart Kahmer,	Philad'a,	Sep'r	23d, 1764
John Mangen,	do.	Sep'r	9th, 1764
Frederick Shenkell,	do.	Sep'r	23d, 1764
Matthias Gebler,	Passyunk,	do.	
George Weck,	Philad'a,	do.	
Godfried Lehr,	Passyunk,	do.	
John Ernst Hayser,	Philadelphia,	do.	
George Justus,	do.	do.	
William Fox,	do.	do.	
Henry Rinehart,	do.	Sep'r	23d, 1764
Henry Gamper,	Blockley,	do.	
George Plum,	Philad'a,	do.	
William Miller,	do.	do.	
Michael Wein,	do.	do.	
John Stroop,	do.	do.	
Michael Mildeberger,	do.	Sep'r	9th, 1764
Jacob Kutch,	Passyunk,	do.	
John Gardner,	Germantown,	Sept.	23, 1764
Matthias Heiss,	Cheltenham,	do.	
Balthaser Ernst,	do.	do.	
Jacob Bare,	Philad'a,	Sep'r	23d, 1764
Bernhard Roop,	do.	do.	
Matthew Waltir,	Marlborough,	Sep'r	16th, 1764
William Bauccus,	North'n Liberties,	Sep'r	23d, 1764
John Rudolph Kohler,	do.	do.	
Thomas Meyer,	Philad'a,	Sep'r	9th, 1764
Casper Glockner,	Passyunk,	Sep'r	23d, 1764
Philip Klumberg,	Philad'a,	do.	
George Losh,	North'n Lib'ties,	Sep'r	24th, 1764
Adam Haas,	Germantown,	do.	
David Heim,	North'n Lib'ties,	do.	
Jacob Mitshed,	do.	Sep'r	23d, 1764
George Scheffer,	Germantown,	Sept.	16th, 1764

Foreigners' names.	Township.	Sacrament, when taken.	
Deitrick Rees,	Philad'a,	Sep'r	9th, 1764
Lewis Hess,	do.	Sep'r	23d, 1764
Henry Smith,	do.	do.	
Jacob Daubendisteil,	do.	do.	
Martin Worn,	do.	do.	
John Gerlach,	do.	do.	
Matthew Kern,	Cushehoppen,	Sep'r	24th, 1764
Balthazar Smidt,	Philad'a,	Sep'r	23d, 1764
Christian Mincke,	Southwark,	do.	
George Doctor,	Upper Salford,	do.	
Philip Ulrich,	Blockley,	do.	
Christian Deitrick,	Philad'a,	Sep'r	9th, 1764
Andrew Bowshard,	do.	do	
Casper Gyer,	do.	Sep'r	23d, 1764
Frederick Schreyer,	do.	Sep'r	9, 1764
Eva Catharina Schlich-			
tern,	do.	Sep'r	9th, 1764
Conrad Schneider,	do.	Sep'r	23d, 1764
Moses Mordecai,	do.	A Jew.	

Lancaster County.

Jacob Frelick,	Lancaster,	August	5th, 1764
George Kemmell,	do.	Sep'r	2d, 1764
Francis Peter Lohrens,	do.	August	5, 1764
George Gerlach,	do.	do.	
John Kehler,	do.	do.	
George Aache,	Cocalico,	Sep'r	20th, 1764
Henry Aache,	do.	Sep'r	15th, 1764
Michael Kissinger,	do.	Sep'r	9th, 1764
David Etelin,	Paxton,	July	22d, 1764
Melchior Gysert,	do.	do.	
Peter Meng,	Heidleberg,	Sep'r	23d, 1764
John Lahn,	do.	do.	
Adam Mengs,	Lebanon,	do.	
Francis Smith,	Heidleberg,	do.	
George Ulrich,	do.	Aug't	12th, 1764
Jacob Fotler,	do.	do.	
Jacob Beck,	Cocalico,	Sep'r	2d, 1764
Jacob Bylestine,	Bart,	Sep'r	3d, 1764
Peter Popp,	Brecknock,	Sep'r	9th, 1764
Conrad Popp,	do.	do.	
Casper Deal,	Carnarvon,	do.	
Henry Siechrist,	Rapho,	Aug't	5th, 1764
Adam Staiger,	Lebanon,	Aug't	29th, 1764
Martin Elie,	do.	Aug't	26th, 1764

Foreigners' names.	Township.	Sacrament, when taken.	
Martin Oberlin,	Bethel,	Aug't	26th, 1764
Sebastian Nagle,	do.	do.	
Frederick Hubley,	Lancaster,	Sep r	2d, 1764
Nicholas Hauer,	do.	Aug't	5th, 1764
Jacob Hildebrand,	do.	Aug't	20th, 1764
Charles Klug,	do.	do.	
Nicholas Ritenauer,	do.	Aug't	5th, 1764
Quirinus Morner,	Brecknock,	Sep'r	24th, 1764
Justus Dreber,	Lancaster,	Aug't	5th, 1764
John Beck,	do.	Sep'r	23d, 1764
Christian Ritz,	do.	do.	
George Schanck,	do.	Sep'r	8th, 1764

Berks County.

Frederick Sinsel,	Oley,	August	23d, 1764
Daniel Schneyder,	Bethel,	Aug't	12th, 1764
Adam Krierchbaum,	Tulpehocken,	do.	
Sebastian Brossius,	do.	do.	
Abraham Scheider,	do.	do.	
Peter Kreitzer,	do.	do.	
Nicholas Gebhard,	Bethel,	do.	
Frederick Hoffman,	Tulpehocken,	do.	
Henry Holtzman,	do.	do.	
George Weikart,	do.	do.	
Philip Wirth,	Union,	Sep'r	23d, 1764
Jacob Wiest,	Oley,	do.	
Jacob Nagle,	do.	Aug't	29th, 1764
John Jordan,	do.	do	
George Merkell,	Richmond,	Sep'r	20th, 1764
Christopher Wiegel,	Douglass,	Sep'r	24th, 1764
John Ritenauer,	Tulpehocken,	Sep'r	12th, 1764
John Henry Smith,	do.	Sep'r ·	24th, 1764

Bucks County.

Manus Weber,	Rockland,	Aug't	20th, 1764
Jacob Dentzeller,	do.	Aug't	2d, 1764

Chester County.

Christopher Knower,	East Nantmele,	July	15th, 1764
Burkhard Becktel,	do.	July	11th, 1764
Godfried Towenhower,	Coventry,	Sep'r	23d, 1764

York County.

Chas. Frederick Wild-bahne,	Heidleburg,	Sep'r	18th, 1764

Foreigners names.	*Township.*	*Sacrament, when taken.*	
Anthony Rietz.	York,	Aug't	27th, 1764
George Eisenhard,	do.	do.	
Adam Partmess,	Dover,	Sep'r	16th, 1764
Ludwic Spies,	do.	Aug't	12th, 1764
Daniel Dinckle,	York,	Sept'r	23d, 1764

The Persons hereafter named being Foreigners, and of the People called Quakers, and other Protestants who conscientiously scruple to take an Oath, severally took the Affirmation and made and repeated the Declaration according to the Directions of the Act of the thirteenth of King George the Second, entituled "An act for naturalizing such foreign Protestants, and others therein mentioned, as are settled or shall settle in any of his Majesty's Colonies in America," and of an Act of General Assembly of the Province of Pennsylvania, made in the Year of our Lord one thousand Seven hundred & Forty-two.

EDW. SHIPPEN, JR., *Prot.*

Lancaster County.

Foreigners' names.	*Township.*	*Moravians, Sacrament, when taken.*	
Matthew Reezer,	Lancaster,	Sep'r	8th, 1764
Jacob Houser,	Earl.		
Abraham Grove,	Earl.		
Lodwic Stone,	Lancaster.		
Michael Miller,	Cocalico.		
Christopher Righart,	Lancaster.		

Philadelphia County.

Jacob Brown,	Philadelphia.		
George Sheppard,	do.		
David Suldrick,	Lower Merrion.		
Peter May,	Upper Hannover.		
George Rouderbush,	do.		
Jesse Guyger,	Merrion.		
Michael Hogberr,	Upper Hannover.		
John Kosser,	North'n Liberties.		
Jacob Snyder,	Germantown.		
Henry Leppy,	Passyunk.		
Wendel Kingfield,	Lower Merrion.		
Peter Smith,	Germantown.		
Henry Hoffman,	Chestnut Hill.		
John Groff,	Plymouth.		
Jacob Stadler,	Philadelphia,	Sep'r	22d, 1764
John Adolph Gilman,	Germantown.		
Leonard Stoneburner,	do.		
Jacob Weaver,	Northern Liberties.		

Berks County.

Foreigners' names.	Township.	Moravians, Sacrament, when taken.
Philip Kouse,	Oley.	
Henry Kraaff,	Tulpehocken.	
Adam Weaver,	Bensalem.	
Christian Fry,	Springfield.	

Bucks County.

John Taymist,	Lower Milford.	

Northampton County.

Abraham Kryder,	Allentown.	

York County.

Michael Dowdle,	York.	

Cumberland County.

Michael Miller,	Antrim.	
John Bussinberger,	Amwell, Hunterdon, in New Jersey.	
Joseph Smith,	Greenwich, Sussex, in New Jersey.	
John Light,	Pilegrove, Salem, West New Jersey.	

[At a Supream Court held at Philadelphia Before William Allen, William Coleman and Alexander Stedman, Esquires, Judges of the said Court, the tenth Day of April, in the year of our Lord one Thousand Seven Hundred and Sixty-five, between the Hours of nine and Twelve of the Clock in the Forenoon of the same Day the following Persons being Foreigners:]

Philadelphia County.

Foreigners' names.	Township.	Sacrament, when taken
George Meleon,	Moyamensing,	April 7th, 1765
John Rebone,	City of Philad'a,	do.
George Keefer,	do.	8th April, 1765
George Shneck,	do.	9th April, 1765
Joseph Spittal,	Douglass,	7th April, 1765
Wilhelm Goetling,	Philad'a,	do.
Jacob Beener,	do.	do.
George Kiehmly,	do.	9th April, 1765
Henry Fox,	Douglass,	7th April 1765
Peter Mann,	Northern Liberties,	do.
Michael Weaver,	do.	do.
John Weeber,	Philad'a,	7th April, 1765
Philip Sensfelder,	do.	do.
George Streyper,	do.	do.
Jno. Wilhelm Engelfried,	do.	do.
Jacob Fischer,	Cheltenham,	8th April, 1765

Foreigners' names.	*Township.*	*Sacrament, when taken.*	
Joshua Lamparter,	Philad'a,	7th April,	1765
George Shaaf,	do.	do.	
Jacob Row,	do.	do.	
Peter Leash,	Passyunk,	do.	
Ludwick Shittler,	Frederick,	do.	
Stephen Steeselmyer,	do.	9th April,	1765
John Hirt,	Whitemarsh,	7th April,	1765
Philip Young,	Philad'a,	do.	
Jacob Bower,	do.	do.	
Jacob Underkoffer,	Frederick,	17th March,	1765
George Gerster,	Oxford,	7th April,	1765
Philip Fackeroth,	do,	do.	
Baltser Stowss,	Philadelphia.		
Michael Stofflat,	do.	7th April,	1765
Valentine Sailer,	Providence,	14th April,	1765

New Jersey.

Wilhelm Wagner,	of New Jersey,	7th April,	1765
Michael Wolfort,	West New Jersey,	9th April,	1765

York County.

Nicholas Working,	Conewago,	8th April,	1765
Ludwick Kieffer,	Codorus,	7th April,	1765
George Jacob Sheffer,	do.	do.	
John Philip Pentz,	York,	9th April,	1765
Balthasar Goll,	do.	do.	
Peter Gascha,	do.	do.	
Michael Weider,	do.	do.	

Berks County.

Geo. Fred'k Scheffer,	Rockland,	1st April,	1765
Matthias Bastian,	Hereford,	7th April,	1765
Abraham Kisler,	Heidleberg,	do.	
Bartholomew Ziebach,	Tulpehocken,	7th March,	1765
Jacob Spees.	Bethel,	do.	
Charles Bomberger,	Tulpehocken,	do.	
Jacob Seltzer,	Heidleberg,	7th April,	1765
George Cresh,	Douglass,	do.	

Lancaster County.

Jacob And'w Spregher,	Lancaster,	3d March,	1765
Godfried Kline,	do.	8th April,	1765
Matthew Buffenmyer,	Hempfield,	7th April,	1765
Andrew Hammer,	Brecknock,	do.	
John Beck,	do.	do.	
Peter Beck,	Earl,	do.	

Foreigners' names.	Township.	Sacrament, when taken.	
Matthew Gerner,	Earl,	7th April,	1765
Christian Swortsweller,	do.	do.	
Adam German,	do.	do.	
Casper Brunner,	Lancaster,	do.	
Zachâry Barth,	Lampeter,	8th April,	1765
Martin Toreward,	Lancaster,	7th April,	1765
Rev'd John Sigfred			
Gerock,	do.	do.	
Jacob Metzer,	do.	7th April,	1765

Northampton County.

Melchior Stricker,	Forks,	7th April,	1765
Philip Walter,	Macungy.	4th April,	1765
Jacob King,	Lynn,	7th April,	1765
George Shreeder,	Weissenberg,	do.	

Bucks County.

Jacob Awlem,	Haycock,	8th April,	1765
Valentine Philip,	Rockland,	do.	
Nicholas Popp,	Bedminster,	5th April,	1765
Henry Bouquet, Colonel in the Royal American Reg't,		3d March,	1765

———

[The Persons hereafter named, being Foreigners, and of the People called Quakers and others who conscientiously scruple the taking an Oath, severally took the Affirmations, and did make & repeat the Declaration according to the Directions of the Act of the Thirteenth of George the Second, entituled "An Act for naturalizing such foreign Protestants and others therein mentioned as are settled or shall settle in any of his Majesty's Colonies in America," and of an Act of General Assembly of the Province of Pennsylvania made in the Year of our Lord one Thousand Seven Hundred and Forty-Two:]

York County.

Foreigners' names.	Township.
Adam Shellich,	Paradise.
Jacob Kuntz,	Germany.
Peter Freed,	York.
Andrew Lantz,	Harlem.

Philadelphia County.

Reudolph Huber,	City of Philad'a.
Joseph Funk,	Northern Liberties.
Michael Feedlee,	New Hannover.
Paul Engle,	Germantown.

Foreigners' names.	Township.	Moravians, Sacrament, when taken.	
Jacob Beiser,	Hatfield.		
Adam Smith,	do.		
Martin Shlatter,	Upper Merrion.		
Casper Rawn,	New Providence.		
Christopher Gideon Myrtetus,	Philad'a,	23d March,	1765
Anthony Lichtel,	Upper Salford,	7th April,	1765
Michael Beard,	Providence.		
Henry Kirtz,	Philad'a.		
Nicholas Workhiser,	Worcester.		
	Bucks County.		
Peter Reppert,	New Britain.		
Henry Hoober,	Lower Milford,	7th April,	1765
John Hornecker,	Rockland.		
	Berks County.		
Valentine Kime,	Maiden Creek.		
Wyrick Selser,	Tulpehocken.		
	Northampton County.		
Anthony Osshyer,	Easton.		
George Rychart,	Lower Saucon.		
	Chester County.		
Adam Richards,	East Caln.		
	Lancaster County.		
Jacob Conrad,	Lebanon.		

[At a Supream Court held at Philadelphia, for the Province of Pennsylvania, before William Allen, William Coleman, and Alexander Stedman, Esquires, Judges of the same Court, the tenth day of April, in the Year of our Lord one thousand seven hundred & sixty-six, between the hours of nine and twelve of the Clock in the forenoon of the same day, the following persons being foreigners:]

Berks County.

Jurors' names.	Township.	Sacrament, when taken.	
Peter Huett,	Exeter,	10th April,	1766
	Philadelphia County.		
Peter Heims,	Philadelphia,	30 March,	1766
Leonard Werntz,	North'n Liberties,	30 do.	
	Northampton County.		
Nich's Lantz,	Williams,	29 March,	1766

And the persons hereafter named, being foreigners, and of the people called Quakers and other Protestants, who conscientiously scruple the taking an oath, severally took the Affirmations & made and subscribed the Declaration according to the directions of the same Act, entitled "An Act for naturalizing such Foreign Protestants and others therein mentioned as are settled or shall settle in any of his Majesty's Colonies in America," and of an Act of General Assembly of this province of Pennsylvania, made in the year of our Lord one thousand seven hundred & forty-two.

EDWARD SHIPPEN, JR., *prot.*

Affirmers' names.	County.	Province.
Peter Kappa,	Hunterdon,	New Jeresy.
Peter Young,	do	do.
Yost Sheffer,	do.	do.
Peter Clover,	do.	do.
John Smith,	do.	do.

[At a Supream Court held at Philadelphia, Before William Allen, William Coleman and Alexander Stedman, Esquires, Judges of the said Court, on the twenty-fourth Day of September, in the Year of our Lord one thousand seven hundred and sixty-six, between the Hours of nine and twelve of the Clock in the Forenoon of the same day, the following Persons, being Foreigners:]

Lancaster County.

Jurors' names.	Township.	Sacrament, when taken.	
Tobias Dittis,	Salisbury,	7th Sept.,	1766
Casper Sheibele,	Lancaster,	2d July,	1766
John Miller,	Earl,	23d Sept.,	1766
Christopher Hanly,	do.	do.	
Dietrick Mareky,	Heidleberg,	21st Sept.,	1766

Berks County.

Philip Kramer,	Reading,	21st Sept.,	1766
Frederick Ulrick,	Rockland,	16th Sept.,	1766
Leonard Keplinger,	Cumry,	22d Sept.,	1766
Jacob Kiesling,	Bern,	do.	
George Kiesling,	do.	do.	
George Dannahower,	Robinson,	21st Sept.,	1766

Bucks County.

Yost Erdman,	Lower Milford,	14th Sept.,	1766

Chester County.

John Carr,	Whiteland,	24th Sept.,	1766
Philip Super,	Haverford,	Oct. 5th,	1766

Philadelphia County.

Michael Gratz,	Philadelphia,	(a Jew.)

Michael Gratz, being a Jew, was qualified & subscribed the Declarations, &c., according to the Directions of the act of the thirteenth of King George the second aforementioned.

The Persons hereafter named, being Foreigners, and of the

People called Quakers, and other Protestants who conscientiously scruple to take an Oath, severally took the affirmation and made and repeated the Declaration according to the Directions of the act of the thirteenth of King George the Second, entituled "an Act for naturalizing such foreign Protestants and others therein mentioned as are settled or shall settle in any of his Majesty's Colonies in American," and of an act of General Assembly of the province of Pennsylvania, made in the Year of our Lord one thousand seven hundred and forty-two.

EDW. SHIPPEN, Jr., *prot.*

Affirmers' names.	*Affirmers' names.*
Martin Reyly,	Jacob Geezy,
Samuel Harnish,	Jacob Albrecht,
Nicholas Harvick,	Daniel Taylor,

Ludwick Hibner, Bethlehem, in Northampton County.

[At a Supream Court held at Philadelphia, Before William Coleman & Alexander Stedman, Esquires, Judges of the said Court, in the tenth Day of April, in the Year of our Lord one thousand seven hundred and sixty-seven, between the Hours of nine and twelve of the Clock in the Forenoon of the same Day, the following Persons being Foreigners:]

Lancaster County.

Jurors' names.	Township.	Sacrament, when taken.	
David Epler,	Earl,	5th April,	1767
Abraham Bollman,	Heidleberg,	do.	
Adam Bach,	Lebanon,	do.	
Jacob Morehard,	Earl,	10th April,	1767
George Potts,	Bethel,	5th April,	1767

Berks County.

Christopher Lerck,	Heidleberg,	5th April,	1767
Peter Sohl,	do.	6th April,	1767
Paul Geiger,	Robinson,	29th March,	1767
Stephen Franciscus Walck,	do.	do.	

Philadelphia County.

Elias Lewis Treichel,	Philadelphia,	9th April,	1767
Peter Kabel,	Marlborough,	7th April,	1767
George Tressly,	Lower Dublin,	8th April,	1767

The Persons hereafter named, being Foreigners, and of the People called Quakers, and other Protestants who conscientiously scruple to take an Oath, severally took the Affirmation and made and repeated the Declaration according to the Directions of the act of the thirteenth of King George the second, entituled "an Act for naturalizing such foreign Protestants and others therein mentioned as are settled or shall settle in any of his Majesty's Colonies in America," and of an Act of General Assembly of the Province of Pennsylvania, made in the year of our Lord one thousand seven hundred and forty-two:

EDW. SHIPPEN, JR., *prot.*

Affirmers' names.	Township.	County.
Augustus Shubart,	Philad'a,	Philad'a.
Casper Shell,	Donegal,	Lancaster.
Philip Hammersmith,	Douglass,	Philadelphia.
Michael Bower,	Amity,	do.
Adam Shyer,	Exeter,	do.
Henry Wacks,	Alsace,	do.
Peter Wacks,	Bern,	do.
Peter Wingleblegh,	Bethel,	Lancaster.
Michael Sights,	Bedminster,	Chester.
John Peter Runyoe,	do.	Bucks.
Stephen Ulrick,	Frederick County, in Maryland.	
Jacob Stutzman,	Cumberland County.	
Michael Miller,	Frederick County, in Maryland.	
Conrad Fox,	do.	
Jacob Shnyder,	do.	
Simon Stucky,	do.	
Philip Jacob Miller,	do.	

[At a Supream Court held at Philadelphia, for the Province of Pennsylvania, before William Allen, William Coleman, John Lawrence and Thomas Willing, Esquires, Judges of the said Court, on the twenty-fourth & twenty-fifth days of September & fifth day of October, in the year of our Lord One Thousand seven hundred and sixty-seven, Between the Hours of nine and twelve of the Clock, in the Forenoon of the same Day, the following Persons, being Foreigners:]

Lancaster County.

Foreigners' names.	Township.	Sacrament, when taken.	
William Kurtz,	Earl,	23d Sept.,	1767

Berks County.

David Fookes,	Reading,	30th August,	1767
John George Woolff,	Tolpehocken,	16th Sept'r,	1767
Conrad Moore,	Robeson,	24th Sept'r,	1767

York County.

Foreigners' names.	Township.	Sacrament, when taken.	
Jacob Michel,	York,	2d August,	1767

Northampton County.

John Adam Miller,	Plainfield,	5th July,	1767
John Nicholas Miller,	do.	do.	
Frederick Limbach,	Upper Milford,	21st Sept'r,	1767
John Greeseman,	Whitehall,	13th Sept'r.	1767
Peter Fookes,	Macungy,	19th Sept'r,	1767
John Miller,	North'n,	13th Sept'r.	1767

Chester County.

John Paul,	Vincent,	20th Sept'r,	1767
Henry Shenckell,	Coventry,	do.	
Jacob Schuster,	Nantmill,	do.	
Henry Shaver,	Charlestown,	6th Sept'r,	1767

Philadelphia County.

John Growar,	Lower Merion,	22d Sept'r,	1767
Leonard Heidley,	do.	do.	
Gideon Moore,	Upper Hanover,	10th Sept'r,	1767
John Woolman,	Horsham,	24th Sept'r,	1767
Conrad Wonnemacher,	New Hanover,	July,	1767
Leonard Weber,	Gwinith,	12th July,	1767
Martin Miller,	Merion,	30th Sept'r,	1767

Bucks County.

Andrew Ziegerfoos,	Springfield,	23d Sept'r,	1767

New Castle County.

Andrew Loynan,		24th Sept'r,	1767

The persons hereafter named, being Foreigners, & of the People called Quakers & other Protestants, who conscientiously scruple to take an Oath, severally took the Affirmation & made & repeated the Declaration according to the Directions of the act of the thirteenth of King George the second, entituled "An Act for naturalizing such foreign Protestants & others therein mentioned as are settled or shall settle in any of his Majesty's Colonies in America," and of an Act of General Assembly of the Province of Pennsylvania, made in the year of our Lord one thousand seven hundred and forty-two:

Foreigners' names.	Township.	County.
Henry Miller,	City of Philad'a,	Philad'a,
Dewald Hushaa,	Brecknock,	Lancaster.
Adam Hynicky,	York,	York.
Wendel Seibert,	Bethel,	Berks.
Christopher Steel,	Manheim,	York.

Foreigners' names.	TownshiC.	County.
Peter Grerard,	Upper Milford,	North'n.
Michael Hirsh,	Lebanon,	Lanc'r.
Peter Smith,	Bethel,	do.
Stophel Knebbell,	do.	Berks.
Stophel Reyer,	do.	do.
Jacob Werryfields,	Frederick County,	in Maryland.
Jacob Bowman,	do.	
Christian Whitmore,	do.	
John Yeager,	do.	
Henry Inkle,	do.	
Samuel Wolegamode,	do.	
Paul Westerberger,	do.	
Christopher Zimmerman,	City of Philad'a,	Philad'a.
William Claus,	Upper Dublin,	Philad'a.

John Cornman, (Moravian,) City of Philad'a, took Sac't 8th Aug't, 1767.

[At a Supream Court held at Philadelphia, for the Province of Pennsylvania, before William Allen, John Lawrence and Thomas Willing, Esqires, Judges of the said Court, on the eleventh day of April, in the year of our Lord one thousand seven hundred and sixty-eight, Between the Hours of nine and twelve of the Clock in the forenoon of the same Day, the following Persons, being foreigners:]

Philadelphia County.

Foreigners' names.	Township.	Sacrament, when taken.	
Conrad Brotzman,	Providence,	1st April,	1768
	Lancaster County.		
Erhard Kliss,	Earl,	11th April,	1768

[At a *Nisi Prius* Court, held at Reading, for the County of Berks, on the thirteenth day of May, in the year of our Lord, one thousand seven hundred and sixty-eight, between the Hours of nine and twelve of the Clock in the forenoon of the same Day, before William Allen, John Lawrence and Thomas Willing, Esquires, Judges of the Supream Court of the Province of Pennsylvania, the following Persons, to wit:]

Berks County.

Foreigners' names who were naturalized at Reading, 13th May, 1768.	Township.	Sacrament, when taken.	
Lawrence Cooper,	Amity,	24th Apr.,	1768
John Reber,	Heidelberg,	10th Apr.,	1768
John Wohlheber,	Tolpohocken,	8th May,	1768
John Jacob,	Bern,	in Easter,	1768
George Michael Kett-			
ner,	Tolpohocken,	11th May,	1768

York County.

Names of foreigners' natur'd at York assizes 20th May, 1768.	Township.	Sacrament, when taken.
Christopher Sliegle, Sen'r,	Berwick,˙	20th May, 1768
Lewis Rudisilly,	Codorus,	do.
Christian Lough,	Manchester,	17th April, 1768
Peter Lough,	do.	do.
Frederick Meyer.	Dover,	27th March, 1768
George Mitchell,	do.	do.
Abraham Bleimyer,	York,	20th May, 1768

Jacob Kurtz, hereafter named being a foreign Protestant, who conscentiously scruples to take an Oath, on the aforesaid thirteenth day of May, before the said Judges of the Supream Court at Reading, in Berks County, aforesaid, took the affirmation and made and repeated the Declaration according to the Directions of the act of the thirteenth of King George the second, intituled "An Act for naturalizing such foreign Protestants and others therein mentioned, as are settled or shall settle in any of his Majesty's Colonies in America," and of an act of General Assembly of the Province of Pennsylvania made in the year of our Lord one thousand seven hundred and forty two:

Affirmers' name.	Township.	County.
Jacob Kurtz,	Cumru,	Berks.

[At a Supream Court held at Philadelphia for the Province of Pennsylvania, Before William Allen, John Lawrence and Thomas Willing, Esquires, Judges of the said Court, the twenty-fourth & twenty-ninth days of September, in the year of our Lord one thousand seven hundred and sixty-eight, between the Hours of nine and twelve of the Clock in the forenoon of the same day, the following Persons being Foreigners:[

Berks County.

Foreigners' names.	Township.	Sacrament, when taken.
Charles Ebersohl,	Reading,	23d Sept'r, 1768
Jacob Neff,	do	do.
Nicholas Smidt,	Colebrookdale,	24th Sept'r, 1768

Philadelphia County.

Michael Swartz,	Upper Dublin,	29th Sept'r, 1768

New Jersey.

William Croft,	Tewksbury, Hunterdon, 23d Sept'r '1768

The Persons hereafter named, being Foreigners, and of the People called Quakers, and other Protestants, who conscien ticusly scruple to take an Oath severally took the affirmation, and made and repeated the Declaration according to the Directions of the act of the thirteenth of King George the second, intituled "an act for the naturalizing such foreign Protestants and others therein mentioned, as are settled or shall settle in any of his Majesty's Colonies, in America," and of an act of General Assembly of the Province of Pennsylvania, made in the year of our Lord One thousand seven hundred and fifty-two.

EDW. SHIPPEN, JR., *prot.*

Northampton County.

Foreigners' names.	Township.	Sacrament, when taken by Moravians.	
John Edwin,	Bethlehem,	13th Aug't,	1768
Ferdinand Jacob Detmers,	do.	10th Sept'r,	1768
John Francis Oberlin,	do.	do.	
John Arbo,	do.	do.	

Chester County.

Jacob Stork,	Ridley.

Frederick County, (in Maryland.)

George Pooderbach.
Catharine Toms.

———

[At a *Nisi prius* Court held at York, for the County of York, Before John Lawrence & Thomas Willing, Esquires, two of the Judges of the Supream Court of the Province of Pennsylvania, on the eighteenth Day of November, in the year of our Lord one thousand seven hundred & sixty-eight.]

York County.

Jurors' names.	Township.	Sacrament, when taken.	
Nicholas Bittinger,	Berwick,	September 18th,	1768
George Swoab,	Paradise,	September 4th,	1768
Philip Christ,	do.	do.	
Daniel Amma,	do.	October 9th,	1768
Adam Kreemer,	Warrington,	October 23d,	1768
Peter Wolf,	Manchester,	October 9th,	1768

[At a *Nisi prius* Court held at York, for the County of York, Before John Lawrence & Thomas Willing, Esquires, two of the Judges of the Supream Court of the Province of Pennsylvania, on the eithteenth Day of November, in the year of our Lord one thousand seven hundred & sixty-eight, Between the Hours of nine & twelve of the Clock in the Forenoon of the same Day, Jacob Lambert, Christian Ratfoun, Adam Dick & Nicholas

Yoner, being Foreigners, & having inhabited & resided for the space of seven years and upwards in his Majesty's Colonies in America, and not having been absent out of some of the said Colonies, for a longer space than two months at any one time during the said seven years, And being severally of the People who conscientiously scruple and refuse the taking an oath, did take & subscribe the affirmations & Declarations.

J. YATES, Cl'k Co'rt N. P.

The Persons before named, having entituled themselves to the Benefit of the Act of Parliament aforesaid, a perfect List of their Names is to be transmitted to the Lords Commissioners for Trade and Plantations; to which End, in pursuance of the said Act, I have caused their their Names to be made known.

THOS. WILLING.

To JOSEPH SHIPPEN, Jr., Esqr., Secretary of the Province of Pennsylvania.

———

[At a Supream Court held at Philadelphia, before William Allen, John Lawrence and Thomas Willing, Esquires, Judges of the said Court, the tenth of April, in the year of our Lord one thousand seven hundred and sixty-nine, between the Hours of nine and twelve of the Clock in the forenoon of the same Day, the following Persons, being Foreigners:]

Bucks County.

Foreigners' names.	Township.	Sacrament, when taken.	
Henry Ruetlinger,	Bristol,	26th March,	1769

Berks County.

John Philip Hasel-becher,	Douglass,	7th April,	1769

Philadelphia County

Ann Mary Dorin,	City of Phil'a,	6th March,	1769

———

[At a *Nisi Prius* Court held at Reading for the county of Berks, before John Lawrence & Thomas Willing, Esquires, two of the Judges of the Supream Court of the Province of Pennsylvania, on the thirtyeth Day of May, in the year of our Lord one thousand seven hundred & sixty-nine:]

Berks County.

Jurors' names.	Township.	Sacrament, when taken	
Michael Schneider,	Heidelberg,	April	23d, 176!
George Geret,	Tulpehocken,	March	26th, 176!

[At a *Nisi Prius* Court held at Carlisle for the County o Cumberland, before John Lawrence & Thomas Willing, Esquires two of the Judges of the Supream Court of the Province of Pennsylvania, on the twenty-second Day of May, in the year of our Lord one thousand seven hundred & sixty-nine:]

Affirmers' name.	*Township.*	*County.*
Michael Hallem,	Antrim,	Cumberland.

[At a *Nisi Prius* Court held at Lancaster, for the County of Lancaster, before John Lawrence & Thomas Willing, Esquires, two of the Judges of the Supream Court of the Province of Pennsylvania, on the sixteenth Day of May, in the year of our Lord one thousand seven hundred & sixty-nine.]

Lancaster County,

Jurors' names.	*Township.*	*Sacrament, when taken.*	
George Dosch,	Mannor,	April	16th, 1769
Jacob Wolf,	Donegal,	March	23d, 1769
Peter Deihl,	Donegal,	March	23d, 1769
Ludwick Lindenmuth,	Donegal,	March	23d, 1769
Philip Brenner,	Donegal,	March	23d, 1769

[At a *Nisi Prius* Court held at Lancaster, for the County of Lancaster, before John Lawrence & Thomas Willing, Esquires, two of the Judges of the Supream Court of the Province of Pennsylvania, on the sixteenth Day of May, in the year of our Lord one thousand seven hundred & sixty-nine.]

Lancaster County.

Affirmers' names.	*Township.*	*Sacrament, when taken by Moravians.*	
Philip Grosh,	Hempfield,	April	22d, 1769
Martin Meixell,	Leacock.		

[At a *Nisi Prius* Court held at York, for the County of York, before John Lawrence & Thomas Willing, Esquires, two of the Judges of the Supream Court of the Province of Pennsylvania, on the twentyeth Day of May, in the Year of our Lord one thousand seven hundred & sixty-nine.]

York County.

Jurors' names.	*Township.*	*Sacrament, when taken.*	
Michael Sparr,	Dover,	April	2d, 1769
Henry Bittinger,	Frederick County, in Virginia,	May	15th 1769

[At a *Nisi Prius* Court held at York, for the County of York, before John Lawrence & Thomas Willing, Esquires, two of the

Judges of the Supream Court of the Province of Pennsylvania, on the twentyeth day of. May, in the Year of our Lord one thousand seven hundred & sixty-nine.]

Affirmers' names.	Township.	County.
Henry Shadron,	York,	York.
Christian Kare,	Manheim,	York.

[At a Supream Court held at Philadelphia, before William Allen, John Lawrence and Thomas Willing, Esq'rs, Judges of the said court, the twenty-fifth of September, in the Year of our Lord one thousand seven hundred and sixty-nine, between the Hours of nine and twelve of the clock in the forenoon of the same Day, the following Persons being Foreigners:]

Bucks County.

Foreigners' names.	Township.	Sacrament, when taken.
Michael Masser,	Nockamixon,	17th Septemb'r 1769
John Phister,	Northampton.	13th August. 1769

[The Persons hereafter named, being Foreigners, and of the People called Quakers, and other Protestants, who conscientiously scruple to take an Oath, severally took the Affirmation and made and repeated the Declaration according to the Directions of an Act of the thirteenth of King George the second, entitled an Act for naturalizing such foreign Protestants and others therein mentioned as are settled or shall settle in any of his majesty's Colonies in America, and of an Act of General Assembly of the Province of Pennsylvania, made in the Year of our Lord one thousand seven hundred and forty-two:]

Foreigners' names.	Township.	County.
Jacob Kieber,	Worcester,	Philadelphia.
John Koke,	Maiden Creek,	Berks.

[At a *Nisi Prius* Court, held at Reading for the County of Berks, before John Lawrence & Thomas Willing, Esquires, two of the Judges of the Supream Court of the Province of Pennsylvania, on the eighteenth Day of November, in the year of our Lord one thousand seven hundred & sixty-nine:]

Philadelphia County.

Jurors' name.	Township.	Sacrament, when taken.
Lubwick Lehman,	Frederick,	October 15th, 1769

[At *Nisi Prius* Court, held at Reading for the County of Berks, before John Lawrence & Thomas Willing, Esquires, two of the Judges of the Supream Court of the Province of Pennsylvania, on the eighteenth Day of November, in the year of our Lord one thousand seven hundred & sixty-nine:]

Affirmers' name.	*Township.*	*County.*
Ludwick Nichola,	Bern,	Berks,

[At a *Nisi Prius* Court held at York for the County of York, before John Lawrence & Thomas Willing, Esquires, two of the judges of the Supream Court of the Province of Pennsylvania, on the twenty-fourth Day of November, in the year of our Lord one thousand seven hundred·and sixty-nine:]

York County.

Jurors' names.	*Township.*	*Sacrament, when taken.*
Tobias Steyer, Senior,	Manheim,	October 19th, 1769
Matthias Hartman,	Dover.	September 3d, 1769

[At a *Nisi Prius* Court held at York, for the County of York, before John Lawrence & Thomas Willing, Esquires, two of the judges of the Supream Court of the Province of Pennsylvania, on the twenty-fourth Day of November, in the year of our Lord one thousand seven hundred & sixty-nine:]

Affirmers' name.	*Township.*	*County.*
John Hagner,	Manchester,	York.

[At a *Nisi Prius* Court, held at Lancaster, for the County of Lancaster, before John Lawrence & Thomas Willing, Esquires, two of the Judges of the Supream Court of the Province of Pennsylvania, on the twenty-second Day of November, in the year of our Lord one thousand seven hundred and sixty-nine:]

Lancaster County.

Jurors' name.		*Sacrament, when taken.*
Peter Koehler,	Borough of Lancaster,	November 1st, 1769

[At a *Nisi Prius* Court held at Lancaster, for the County of Lancaster, before John Lawrence & Thomas Willing, Esquires, two of the Judges of the Supream Court of the Province of Pennsylvania, on the twenty-first Day of November, in the year of our Lord one thousand seven hundred and sixty-nine:]

Affirmers' names.	*Township.*	*County.*
John Stouffer,	Lampeter,	Lancaster.
John Rohrer,	do.	do.

[At a Supream Court held at Philadelphia, for the Province of Pennsylvania, the tenth day of April, in the Year of our Lord one thousand seven hundred and seventy, before William Allen, John Lawrence and Thomas Willing, Esquires, Judges of the said Court, between the Hours of nine and twelve of the Clock in the forenoon of the same day, the following Persons, being foreigners:]

Berks County.

Foreigners' names.	Township.	Sacrament, when taken.	
Andrew Dihm,	Cumry,	10th April,	1770

Northampton County.

Zacharias Haller,   Lindon.

Bucks County.

Henry Leimbacker,   Northampton.

———

[At a *Nisi Prius* Court held at York, for the County of York, before John Lawrence & Thomas Willing, Esquires, two of the Judges of the Supream Court of the Province of Pennsylvania. on the twenty-first Day of May, in the year of our Lord one thousand seven hundred & seventy :]

York County.

Jurors' names'	Township.	Sacrament, when taken.	
Conrad Stuck,	Codorus,	April	29th. 1770
Adam Syfert,	Dover,	May	13th, 1770
Conrad Wisham,	Dover,	April	12th, 1770

———

[At a *Nisi Prius* Court held at York, for the County of York, before John Lawrence & Thomas Willing, Esquires, two of the Judges of the Supream Court of the Province of Pennsylvania, on the twenty-first Day of May, in the year of our Lord one Thousand seven hundred & seventy :]

Affirmers' names.	Township.	County.
Matthias Detter,	Manchester,	York.
Johannes Ermel,	Paradise,	York.

———

[At a *Nisi Prius* Court held at Lancaster. for the County of Lancaster, before John Lawrence & Thomas Willing, Esquires, two of the Judges of the Supream Court of the Province of Pennsylvania, on the seventeenth Day of May, in the year of our Lord one thousand seven hundred & seventy :]

Lancaster County.

Jurors' name.	Township.	Sacrament, when taken.	
John Ludwig,	Earl,	April	29th, 1770

———

[At a *Nisi Prius* Court held at Carlisle, for the County of Cumberland, before John Lawrence & Thomas Willing, Esquires, two of the Judges of the Supream Court of the Province of Pennsylvania, on the twenty-fifth Day of May, in the year of our Lord one thousand seven hundred & seventy :]

Affirmers' name.
Lawrence Shook, of Frederick county, in Maryland.

[At a Supream Court held at Philadelphia for the province of Pennsylvania, before William Allen, John Lawrence and Thomas Willing, Esquires, Judges of the same Court, the twenty-fourth day of September, in the Year of our Lord one thousand seven hundred and seventy, between the Hours of nine and twelve of the clock in the forenoon of the same day, the following Persons being Foreigners:]

Foreyners' names.	Township.	County.	Sacr't, when taken.
Jacob Heisler,	Gwinedth,	Philad'a	2d Sept.,	1770
George Barge,	City of Philadelphia,	24th Sept.,	1770
Jacob Miller,	Bethlehem, Hunterdon, in New Jersey,	do.
Levy Marks,	City of Philadelphia, a Jew.
John Conrad Gregg,	Newport,	New Castle,	1st Sept., 1770

The persons hereafter named being Foreigners, and of the people called Quakers and other Protestants who conscientiously scruple to take an Oath, severally took the affirmation & made & repeated the Declaration according to the Directions of the Act of the thirteenth of King George the Second, entitled "an Act for Naturalizing such Foreign Protestants & others therein mentioned, as are settled or shall settle in any of his Majesty's Colonies in America," and of an Act of General Assembly of the Province of Pennsylvania, made in the year of our Lord one thousand seven hundred and forty-two.

EDW. SHIPPEN, Jr., prot.

Foreigners' names.	Township.	County.
Wendel Dantfeltzer,	Nantmill,	Chester.
Peter Wenger,	do.	do.
John Mingle,	Oxford,	Sussex, in New Jersey.
Peter King,	Hatfield,	Philad'a.
Jacob Diemer,	Earl,	Lancaster.
Jacob Freich,	Nockamixon, Bucks.
George Grauss,	Coventry,	Chester.

[At a *Nisi Prius* Court held at Reading, for the County of Berks, Before John Lawrence & Thomas Willing, Esquires, two of the Judges of the Supream Court of the Province of Pennsylvania, on the nineteenth Day of November, in the Year of our Lord one thousand seven hundred and seventy.]

Jurors' name.	Township.	County.	Sacrament, when taken
Andreas Kachel,	Cumru,	Berks,	September 30, 1770

[At a *Nisi Prius* Court held at Lancaster, for the County of Lancaster, before John Lawrence and Thomas Willing, Esquires, two of the Judges of the Supreme Court of the Province of Pennsylvania, on the twenty-first Day of November, in the year of our Lord one thousand seven hundred and seventy.]

Lancaster County.

Jurors' names.	Township.	Sacrament, when taken.
Jacob Hollinger,	Borough of Lancaster,	November 18th, 1770
Michael Krehl,	Bethel,	October 14th, 1770
Arnold Shervitz,	Hannover,	October 14th, 1770
Henry Schmidt,	Hempfield,	November 18th, 1770

[At a *Nisi Prius* Court held at Lancaster, for the County of Lancaster, before John Lawrence & Thomas Willing, Esquires, two of the Judges of the Supream Court of the Province of Pennsylvania, on the twenty-first day of November, in the year of our Lord one thousand seven hundred and seventy.]

Affirmers' name.	Township.	County.
Simon Schneider,	Of the borough of Lancaster,	Lancaster.

[At a Supream Court held at Philadelphia, for the Province of Pennsylvania, the Eleventh day of April, in the Year of our Lord one thousand seven hundred & seventy-one, before John Lawrence and Thomas Willing, Esquires, Judges of the said Court, between the hours of nine and twelve of the Clock in the forenoon of the same day, the following persons, being foreigners.]

Philadelphia County.

Foreigners' names.	Township.	Sacrament, when taken
William Clauer,	City of Phil'a,	31st March, 177
Philipina Waggoner,	do.	do.
John Fritz,	Douglass,	10th Ap'l, 177
Lewis Stannert,	Whitemarsh,	7th Ap'l, 177
Charles Leopold,	do.	10th Ap'l, 177
Andreas Maurer,	New Cushahoppen,	31st March, 177
Lewis Farmer,	City of Philadelphia,	do.

Berks County.

Peter Lober,	Colebrookdale,	7th Ap'l, 17

Catharine Ikken, hereafter named, being a foreign protestan who conscientiously scruples and refuses to take an oath, too the Affirmation and made and repeated the Declaration accor ing to the directions of the act of the thirteenth of King Geor the second, entituled " An Act for naturalizing such Foreign Pr testants and others as are settled or shall settle in any of h Majesty's Colonies in America," and of an Act of Gener Assembly of the province of Pennsylvania, made in the year our Lord one thousand seven hundred & forty-two.

Name.	Township.	County.
Catharine Ikken,	Upper Milford,	Northampton.

EDW. SHIPPEN, Jr., *prot.*

[At a *Nisi Prius* Court, held at Reading, for the County of Berks, before John Lawrence & Thomas Willing, Esquires, two of the Judges of the Supream Court of the Province of Pennsylvania, on the seventeenth Day of May, in the year of our Lord one thousand seven hundred & seventy-one:]

Berks County.

Jurors' name.	Township.	Sacrament, when taken.
John Hopff,	Tulpehocken,	May 7th, 1771

[At a *Nisi Prius* Court, held at Reading for the County of Berks, before John Lawrence & Thomas Willing, Esquires, two of the Judges of the Supream Court of the Province of Pennsylvania, on the twentyeth Day of May, in the year of our Lord one thousand seven hundred & seventy-one:]

Affirmers' name,	Township,	County.
Andrew Yost,	Brecknock,	Berks.

[At a *Nisi Prius* Court held at Lancaster, for the County of Lancaster, before John Lawrence & Thomas Willing, Esquires, two of the Judges of the Surpeam Court of the Province of Pennsylvania, on the twenty-fourth Day of May, in the Year of our Lord one thousand seven hundred & seventy-one:]

Lancaster County.

Jurors' names.	Township.	Sacrament, when taken.
Nicholas Long,	Lancaster borough,	May 19th, 1771
Jacob Brucker,	Lebanon,	March 31st, 1771
Maurice Duppel,	Heidelberg,	May 21st, 1771

[At a *Nisi Prius* Court held at Lancaster, for the County of Lancaster, before John Lawrence & Thomas Willing, Esquires, two of the Judges of the Supream Court of the Province of Pennsylvania, on the twenty-fourth Day of May, in the Year of our Lord one thousand seven hundred & seventy-one:]

Affirmers' name.	Township.	County.
Peter Shoemaker,	Cocalico.	Lancaster.

[At a *Nisi Prius* Court held at York, for the County of York, before Thomas Willing, Esquire, one of the Judges of the Supream Court of the Province of Pennsylvania, on the thirtieth Day of May, in the year of our Lord one thousand seven hundred and seventy-one:]

York County,

Jurors' names.	Township.	Sacrament, when taken
Frederick Housman,	York,	May 19th, 177
Michael Hemicker,	York,	May 19th, 177
Jacob Probst,	York,	April 31st, 177

[At a *Nisi Prius* Court held at York, for the County of York before Thomas Willing, Esquire, one of the Judges of the Su pream Court of the Province of Pennsylvania, on the thii tieth Day of May in the year of our Lord one thousand seve hundred & seventy-one:]

Affirmers' names.

George Yerkardt, of Frederick county, in Maryland.
Peter Naffseger, of Frederick county, in Maryland.
John George Storm, of Frederick County, in Maryland.

[At a Supream Court held at Philadelphia, for the Provinc of Pennsylvania, before William Allen, John Lawrence an Thomas Willing, Esquires, Judges of the said Court the twenty fourth Day of September, in the year of our Lord one thousan seven hundred and seventy-one, between the hours of nine an twelve of the Clock in the forenoon of the same day, the follov ing person, being a foreigner:]

Philadelphia County.

Name.	Township.	Sacrament, when take
Nicholas Carl,	Upper Dublin,	25th Aug., 17

EDW. SHIPPEN, JR., *Prot.*

The Persons hereafter named being foreign Protestants wh conscientiously scruple to take an Oath, severally took tl Affirmation and made and repeated the Declaration according t the Directions of an act of Parliament made in the thirteent year of the Reign of George the Second, intitled "An act fc naturalizing such foreign Protestants and others therein mei tioned, as are settled or shall settle in any of his Majesty Colonies in America," and of an Act of General Assembly the Province of Pennsylvania, made in the Year of our Loi one thousand Seven hundred & Forty-two.

Foreigners' names.	Township.	County.
Christopher Ricks,	East Caln,	Chester.
Frederick Frees,	Frederick County, in Virginia.	

[At a *Nisi Prius* Court held at Reading, for the County Berks, Before John Lawrence & Thomas Willing, Esquire two of the Judges of the Supream Court of the Province Pennsylvania, on the sixteenth Day of November, in the ye of our Lord one thousand seven hundred & seventy-one:]

Berks County.

Jurors' name.	Township.	Sacrament, when taken.
Adam Behm.	Brecknock,	October 13th, 1771

[At a *Nisi Prius* Court held at Reading for the County of Berks before John Lawrence & Thomas Willing, Esquires, two of the, Judges of the Supream Court of the Province of Pennsylvania, on the sixteenth day of November, in the Year of our Lord one thousand seven hundred & seventy-one:]

Affirmers' name.	Township.	County.
Peter Breyfogel,	Maiden Creek,	Berks.

[At a *Nisi Prius* Court held at Lancaster, for the County of Lancaster, before John Lawrence & Thomas Willing, Esquires, two of the Judges of the Supream Court of the Province of Pennsylvania, on the twenty-third Day of November, in the Year of our Lord one thousand seven hundred and seventy-one.]

Lancaster County.

Jurors' names.	Township.	Sacrament, when taken.
Jacob Decker,	Borough of Lancaster, Septem'r	1st, 1771
Christian Ilgner,	Borough of Lancaster, Octob'r	13th, 1775

[At a Supream Court held at Philadelphia, for the Province of Pennsylvania, before William Allen, John Lawrence and Thomas Willing, Esquires, Judges of the said Court, the tenth Day of April, in the Year of our Lord one thousand seven hundred and seventy-two, between the Hours of nine and twelve of the Clock in the Forenoon of the same Day, the following Persons being Foreigners:]

Philadelphia County.

Foreigners' names.	Township.	Sacrament, when taken.
William Smith,	City of Philadelphia,	5th, April, 1772
John Weber,	Gwinedth,	3d April, 1772
George Renner,	Whitpain,	do,
John Peter Emerick,	Gwinedth,	30th March 1772
Godfrey Reinhard,	Tewksbury, Hunter-	
	don in N. Jersey,	10th April, 1772
Gerard Hulsekamp,	City of Philadelphia,	19th April, 1772

The persons hereafter named, being Foreigners, and of the People called Quakers, and others who conscientiously scruple to take an Oath, severally took the affirmation and made and repeated the Declaration according to the Directions of the act of the thirteenth of George the Second, entituled "an Act for nat-

uralizing such foreign Protestants and others therein mentione
as are settled or shall settle in any of his Majesty's Colonic
in America," and of an act of General Assembly of the pr vinc
of Pennsylvania, made in the Year of our Lord one thousand sev
en hundred and forty-two.

EDW. SHIPPEN, JR., *prot.*

Foreigners' names.	*Township.*	*County.*
John Schott,	Hatfield,	Philadelphia.
John Erdman Dorig,	Monackesie, land.	Frederick County in Mary

---

[At a *Nisi Prius* Court held at Reading, for the County c
Berks, before John Lawrence & Thomas Willing, Esquires, tw
of the Judges of the Supream Court of the Province of Pennsy
vania, on the eighteenth & twentieth Days of May, in the Yea
of our Lord one thousand seven hundred & seventy-two :]

Berks County.

Jurors names.	*Township.*	*Sacrament, when take:*
(May 12th, 1772.)		
Henry Schreffler,	Reading,	April 19th, 177
Nicholas Keller,	Coventry,	April 19th, 177
(May 20th, 1772.)		
Adam Calback,	Tulpehocken,	April 19, 177

[At a *Nisi Prius* Court held at York, for the County of York
before John Lawrence & Thomas Willing, Esquires, two of th
Judges of the Supream Court of the Province of Pennsylvania
on the thirtieth Day of May, in the Year of our Lord one thou
sand seven hundred & seventy-two :]

Jurors' names.	*Township and Province,*	*Sacrament, when taken*
Philip Fishborn Tawney Town, Pipe Creek		
Hundred, Frederick county in Maryland,	May	29th, 177
Michael Huber, Coset's Run, Frederick coun-		
ty in Maryland,	May	29th, 177
Christopher Miller, Pipe Creek Hundred,		
Frederick county in Maryland.	May	30th, 177

[At a *Nisi Prius* Court held at York, for the County of York
before John Lawrence & Thomas Willing, Esquires, two of th
Judges of the Supream Court of the Province of Pennsylvania
on the twenty-ninth & thirtieth Days of May, in the Year o
our Lord one thousand seven hundred & seventy-two :]

Affirmers' names.	*County.*	*Province.*
(May 29, 1770.)		
Christian Bower;	Frederick County,	Maryland.
John Henry David,	Baltimore,	Maryland.
Philip Stombagh,	Frederick,	Maryland.
Michael Beagler,	Codorus Township,	York County.
Nicholas Forney,	Manheim Township,	York County.
Mathias Stehr,	York Town,	York County.
(May 30th, 1772.)		
Henry Worman,	Sam's Creek, Frederick county,	Maryland.

[At a *Nisi Prius* Court held at Lancaster, for the County of Lancaster, before John Lawrence & Thomas Willing, Esquires, two of the Judges of the Supream Court of the Province of Pennsylvania, on the twenty-third day of November, one thousand seven hundred and seventy-three.]

Lancaster County.

Jurors' names.	*Township*	*Sacrament, when taken*
Frederick Sheaffer,	Lancaster borough,	October 31st, 1773

York County.

Gerhard Graeff,	Dover,	October 17th, 1773

[At a *Nisi Prius* Court held at Lancaster, for the County of Lancaster, Before John Lawrence & Thomas Willing, Esquires, two of the Judges of the Supream Court of the Province of Pennsylvania, on the twenty-second, twenty-third and twenty-fourth Days of November, in the Year of our Lord one thousand seven hundred and seventy-three.]

Affirmers' names.	*Township,*	*County.*
Stophel Kreisser	York,	York.
Paul Roodt,	Of Frederick County in Maryland.	
John French,	Colebrookdale,	Berks.
John Baker,	Lancaster Borough,	Lancaster.